Colloquial French

Ça Baigne!

Colloquial French

Ça Baigne!

C.W.E. Kirk-Greene

foulsham

LONDON • NEW YORK • TORONTO • SYDNEY

foulsham

Yeovil Road, Slough, Berkshire SL1 4JH

ISBN 0-572-01533-X

Copyright © 1992 C.W.E. Kirk-Greene

Designed and typeset by
Jeffery White Creative Associates, Oxford, UK.

Printed in Great Britain by St Edmundsbury Press Ltd,
Bury St Edmunds, Suffolk.

Contents

Preface

Many people feel frustrated because they have difficulty in understanding typical, informal, everyday French, even though they have learnt the language to a certain standard. A stumbling block is likely to be the wide use of familiar French.

This book is certainly no exhaustive dictionary but it gives many of the common words and expressions as well as some of special interest. The *Petites Révisions*, which highlight some of the examples, may be useful for refreshing the memory or for self-assessment.

C. K-G.

Acknowledgements ━━━━

I am particularly grateful to my good friends Monsieur C. Kohler and Monsieur J. Garnier for their suggestions, answers and unfailing interest. I also wish to thank very much Mademoiselle Natacha Demianenko, sometime 'lectrice' at the University of Sussex, who most patiently dealt with a a good number of queries.

Harrap's *Slang Dictionary English-French/French-English* (by G. A. Marks and C. B. Johnson completely revised and edited by J. Pratt 1984) and *Dictionary of Modern Colloquial French* by R. J. Hérail and E. A. Lovatt (Routledge & Kegan Paul 1984) have been useful for some checking and I recommend them to those who wish to delve more deeply into the subject. Collins *Robert French Dictionary* (1987) has been useful too. Finally, my thanks are due to my illustrator, and to my supportive editor Dr J. Cox.

Note * especially familiar or slangy French

A

Abandonment

plaquer*	to drop, ditch; to give up, chuck up
envoyer tout promener	to jack it all in
décrocher	to pull out, drop out

*La soixantaine venue, je pense à **décrocher**:* Having reached the sixties I'm thinking of hanging up my boots.

*Ce gosse commence à **décrocher**:* This kid is becoming a drop-out.

jeter l'éponge	to throw in the sponge
mettre les pouces	to give in, cave in

*Il a beau me menacer. Pas question de **mettre les pouces**:* He can go on threatening me. There's no way I am giving in.

lâcher	to let down, pack up

*Ma vieille mobylette est en train de me **lâcher**:* My old moped is packing up on me.

larguer	to jettison, ditch

*Il a **largué** sa petite amie:* He has ditched his girl friend.

planter là	to leave stranded
laisser en rade	

*Bien sûr les touristes ne veulent pas être **laissés en rade** pour la nuit:* Of course the tourists don't want to be stranded for the night.

rester le bec dans l'eau	to be left stuck, nonplussed, frustrated
pouce!	pax! (as children used to say in their games) I surrender! enough!

Abandonment

déclarer forfait — to pull out (properly to scratch in sport)

*Enfin devant tant d'obstacles mon chauffeur **déclara forfait**:* Finally faced by so many obstacles my driver packed it in.

claquer la porte — to leave, walk out in a huff

mettre la clé sous la porte, sous le paillasson — to shut up shop, close down, call it a day (with the image of leaving the key under the mat)

mettre au clou — to retire, hang up one's boots

*Notre meilleur tennisman **a mis** sa raquette **au clou**:* Our best tennis player has hung up his racket.

n'avoir que ses yeux pour pleurer — to be left with nothing

*Ayant perdu tous ses bagages il **n'avait que ses yeux pour pleurer**:* Having lost all his luggage he was left with nothing.

reprendre ses billes* — to pull out, withdraw (as from an agreement)

*Au lieu de signer le contrat j'ai **repris mes billes**:* Instead of signing the contract I pulled out.

faire son deuil de quelque chose — to give something up as lost ('deuil' = mourning)

*Et ce porte-feuille, il peut **en faire son deuil**:* He won't see that wallet again.

faire une croix sur quelque chose — to write something off

*J'ai dû **faire une croix** sur une médaille:* I had to give up any hope of a medal.

donner sa langue au chat   to give up (of a riddle)

Est-ce l'œuf qui a fait la poule ou la poule qui a fait l'œuf?
Je ne sais pas.
Si! Si!
*Non, je **donne ma langue au chat**.*
Et moi aussi:

Which came first, the egg or the chicken?
I don't know.
Yes, you do!
No, I give up.
So do I.

Admiration

ce n'est pas rien   it's no mean feat

*Paris – Nice à pied **ce n'est pas rien**:* Paris – Nice on foot is pretty good going.

(il) faut le faire!   it takes some doing that does!

*Trois victoires de suite, **faut le faire!**:* Three wins on the trot, that takes some doing!

chapeau!   congrats! I take my hat off to you!

Advantages

les bénefs (m)   perks, extras (from 'bénéfices')

*Et encore, il y a **les** petits **bénefs**:* Then there are the perks.

la promo   special offer (from 'promotion')

*Jusqu'à samedi **des promos** sur tous les achats:* Up to Saturday reductions on all purchases.

Age

prendre de la bouteille   to be older and wiser

sucrer les fraises *   to be very shaky and doddery (The image is of a hand shaking sugar onto strawberries.)

rétro   old-style, old-time (from 'rétrograde')

*C'est confortable, avec des meubles **rétro**:* It's comfortable, with old-style furniture.

la soixantaine bien tassée   well into the sixties

*L'ancien champion, **la soixantaine bien tassée**, joue toujours bien:* The former champion, well into his sixties, still plays well.

(être) sur le retour   to be getting on a bit, to be over the top

*Dans son roman il s'agit de deux actrices **sur le retour**:* Her novel is about two actresses who are getting on a bit.

de papa   old-fashioned, dated

*Tu crois que c'est un sport **de papa**?:* You think it's an old-fashioned sport?

le pépé *
le pépère *   old man, dodderer

*Mais vous êtes un jeune homme – pas encore **un pépé**!:* But you're a young chap, not an oldie yet!

*«Tu retardes, **pépère**!» m'a crié le gosse:* 'You're behind the times, grandad!' the kid shouted to me.

la mémé *
la mémère *   old woman

*Que de monde! Et puis j'entends une voix qui crie: «Laissez passer **les mémères**!»:* What a crowd! And then I hear a voice shout: 'Let the old dears through!'

les croulants * (m)	old fogeys ('crouler' = to collapse, crumble)
jouer les jeunots	to pretend to be one of the young

Agreement

d'ac * ça colle	OK, agreed, right! (from 'd'accord')

*«On sort ce soir?» «**D'ac**!»*: 'Shall we go out tonight?' 'OK!'

***Ça colle** pour dimanche?*: All right for Sunday?

banco!	you're on! It's a deal!

Ambition

un jeune loup	an ambitious young man who is going places (especially politics and business)

***Un jeune loup** de la finance*: A financial whiz kid.

avoir les dents longues	to be hungry for success

*De nos jours ils nous faut du personnel **aux dents longues***: Nowadays we need ambitious staff.

en vouloir *	to want to get on

*Il **en veut** celui-là*: There's a chap who's itching to succeed.

Amusement / pleasure

la télé telly
la téloche *

*Une soirée de relax devant **la télé**:* An evening of relaxation in front of the telly.

la boîte à images the 'box'
la petite boîte

le feuilleton mélo 'soap' ('mélo' from 'mélodramatique')

le bouquin book (In standard French 'bouquiniste' is a secondhand bookseller especially in Paris along the banks of the Seine.)

la B.D. comic strip, cartoon (from 'bande dessinée') (Comics have a considerable following in France.)

le polar * thriller (book, film)

*L'inspecteur remarqua tout de suite quelques **polars** qui traînaient sur la table basse:* The detective immediately noticed a few thrillers lying about on the coffee table.

l'hebdo (m) weekly (paper) (from 'hebdomadaire')

la feuille de chou rag, paper
le canard

*Elle est journaliste dans une **feuille de chou locale**:* She's a journalist on a local rag.

la diapo slide (from 'diapositive')

le ciné cinema

*On va au **ciné**?:* Shall we go and see a film?

le cinoche * cinema, flicks

Le cinoche préféré de ma jeunesse en centre-ville n'est plus là: The favourite cinema of my youth in the town centre is no longer there.

tâter de (la photographie) to have a go at (photography)

la boum party, fling (especially for the
la surboum younger set)
la surpatte *

*Je l'ai vue dans une de ces **boums**: I saw her at one of these parties.*

s'éclater * to let one's hair down

*Le weekend **je m'éclate**:* At the weekend I have a high old time.

se défouler to let off steam

***Je me défoule** en jouant au squash:* I switch off completely by playing squash.

décompresser to relax with the pressure off, to wind down

*Pour **décompresser** elle aime passer le weekend au bord de la mer:* To get away from it all and really relax she likes to spend the weekend by the sea.

se mettre les pieds sous to put one's feet up (The French
la table prefer to keep them *under* the table.)

se la couler douce * to have a really easy, carefree time, to have it made

se baguenauder to stroll around

prendre un bol d'air to go out for a breather

faire une balade to go for a walk, drive, trip
se balader

*J'aime **me balader** en solitaire dans la forêt:* I like walking alone in the forest.

Amusement / pleasure

faire une virée to go for a jaunt, outing

Ils font du lèche-vitrines

lécher les vitrines to go window-shopping
faire du lèche-vitrines

guincher * to dance, shake a leg

en guincher une * to have a dance, a spin

le bœuf jam session

rigoler to have fun, a laugh
se marrer*

*Nous étions cinq et on a bien **rigolé** samedi soir:* There were five of us and we had good fun on Saturday night.

marrant * hilarious, a scream

c'est astap! * it's an absolute hoot! (from 'à se taper le derrière par terre')

s'en payer une tranche to have a high old time

la boîte night club (from 'boîte de nuit')

*Ils aiment courir **les boîtes**:* They like to go round the night clubs.

faire la bringue *	to go on the razzle
faire la tournée des grands ducs	to have a night out, to hit the top spots (as might have been enjoyed by the grand dukes)
faire de la bronzette	to enjoy a spot of sunbathing
faire du ski-bar	to enjoy the non-skiing pleasures of winter sports (drinking, dancing)
pas folichon	not much fun

*Sa vie n'est **pas folichonne**:* She doesn't have much of a life.

To Annoy

casser les pieds à quelqu'un	to annoy, bore someone

*Il **me casse les pieds**:* He's an absolute pest.

tu me les casses! *	you're a real pain!
mettre quelqu'un en boule	to infuriate someone, to put someone's hackles up
mettre quelqu'un en boîte	to take the mickey out of someone, to wind someone up
faire tourner quelqu'un en bourrique	to drive someone round the bend
faire râler quelqu'un	to make someone livid

*C'est ça qui **fait râler** les étudiants:* That's what infuriates the students.

faire bondir quelqu'un	to make someone hopping mad, really furious

*L'expression 'vieille fille' **me fait** toujours **bondir**:* The expression 'old maid' always makes me hopping mad.

faire suer quelqu'un	to bore someone, to be a pain to someone

To Annoy

faire chier quelqu'un * to sicken someone

donner des boutons à to annoy, give someone the pip
quelqu'un

*La musique de chambre **me donne des boutons**:* I can't get on with chamber music.

Appearance/build

l'escogriffe (m) lanky fellow

un gros lard * a fat lump
un gros plein de soupe *

bâti en armoire à glace built like a wardrobe (from 'armoire à glace' = wardrobe)

*Tu vois le genre? Un rugbyman **bâti en armoire à glace**:* You know the type? A great hefty rugby player.

le gabarit build

*On admire son **gabarit** d'athlète:* One admires his athletic build.

costaud tough, chunky

*Un type **costaud** est là pour filtrer les visiteurs:* A hefty chap is there to check out the visitors.

balèze * strong, burly

rouquin red-haired

avoir l'air tristounet to look 'down', to look rather sorry for oneself

(un air) BCBG a smart, classy Sloane Rangerish look (BCBG comes from 'Bon Chic Bon Genre') (The expression can also be used of things.)

*Son charme **BCBG** a séduit tout le monde:* His easy and assured charm won over everyone.

bien baraqué well built

à poil, naked, 'starkers' (It is important
dans le plus simple not to confuse 'à poil', and 'au
appareil poil' = super.)

avoir une bonne tête to look like a good sort

on avait l'air fin! we looked proper Charlies!
on avait l'air instruit!

*Si cela arrivait on aurait **l'air instruit**!:* If that happened we would look complete idiots!

avoir une gueule to look really sick, down in the
d'enterrement mouth

binoclard wearing spectacles ('binoclard' is also used as a noun)

*Un jeune Anglais **binoclard** me regardait fixement:* A young English chap with specs was staring at me.

déglingué falling to bits, ramshackle

*Un vieux taxi **déglingué** nous attendait:* A ramshackle old taxi was waiting for us.

Appointment

le rencart * date, meeting

*On peut être sûr que c'est **un rencart** qu'il ne va pas manquer:* One can be sure this is an appointment he is not going to miss.

Appreciation

c'est à se mettre à genoux — it's marvellous

*Vos martinis sont **à se mettre à genoux**!:* Your martinis are heavenly!

ce n'est pas de la petite bière — it's not unimportant, it's not to be sneezed at

ce n'est pas de refus — I won't say no

*Une coupe de champagne? **Ce n'est pas de refus**:* A glass of champagne? I won't say no.

ne pas cracher sur quelque chose — not to turn up one's nose at something
ne pas faire la fine bouche

*Mille francs si je le fais? **Je ne crache pas dessus**:* A thousand francs if I do it? I won't turn my nose up at that.

*Bien sûr je ne vais **pas faire la fine bouche** sur une médaille de bronze:* Of course I am not going to turn my nose up at a bronze medal.

ne pas cracher dans la soupe — not to be ungrateful for an offer, not to spurn something

*Il veut me prêter sa bagnole. Eh bien, je ne vais pas **cracher dans la soupe**:* He wants to lend me his car. Well, I'm not saying no to that.

ça vaut le coup — it's well worthwhile
ça vaut le jus *

Approximation

chercher dans — to be about, to run into (figures)

*C'est cher. Ça va **chercher dans** les huit mille francs:* It's expensive. It'll run into eight thousand francs.

à tout casser   at the outside

*Mille réfugiés, **à tout casser**, sont partis. Il faut encore s'occuper des autres:* A thousand refugees, at the outside, have left. We must still look after the rest.

à vue de nez   roughly, at a guess
au pif *
au pifomètre *

***Au pif** je dirais un ancien prof:* Taking a long shot I'd say an ex-teacher.

et le pouce!   and a bit more!

*Il a soixante ans. **Et le pouce!**:* He's sixty. Over that!

et des poussières   just over, past (numerals, time)

*Elle est revenue à minuit **et des poussières**:* She got back just after midnight.

et quelque   and a bit

*A la page cinquante **et quelque**:* On page fifty something.

Argument

il n'y a pas à tortiller	there's no getting away from it
y mettre son grain de sel	to shove in one's oar, have one's say
ne pas pouvoir en placer une *	not to be able to get in a word edgeways
des discussions de marchands de tapis	haggling (the image of the pavement rug sellers who tempt you to buy)
ramener sa fraise * **la ramener** *	to butt in, protest, become stroppy

*Ensuite ils m'ont menacé. «Si vous **la ramenez**, on vous tabasse. Compris?»:* Then they threatened me. 'If you kick up a fuss we'll beat you up. Got it?'

Argument

t'occupe! *

you mind your own damn business! you keep out of this! (as impolite as it is curt with its omission of the negative. The expression can have a milder sense of 'don't worry, leave it to me'.)

Army/services

la grande muette *

the army

le troufion *

soldier

*Marc, c'est un bon ami. On a été **troufions** ensemble, vous savez:*
Marc is a good friend. We were in the army together, you know.

le bleu

recruit, new bloke, squaddy

le bidasse *

private

le toubib

doc (also widely used in a general context. It is a word of Arabic origin which has been brought over via military slang.)

*«Faites aaah!», dit **le toubib***: 'Say ah!', says the doc.

Le toubib

se faire porter pâle	to report sick
la perm	leave (from 'permission')

*A chaque **perm** je partais pour Paris:* Every leave I'd set off for Paris.

la quille *	demob
le crachat *	medal, gong
la banane *	
la ficelle	stripe
la sardine *	

*Ma troisième **ficelle**!:* My third stripe!

le singe *	bully beef

*Je lui ai tendu une boîte de **singe**:* I offered him a tin of bully beef.

faire la tournée des popotes	to do the rounds (officer)
en pékin *	in civvies

Avarice

être près de ses sous	to be close with one's money
radin	stingy
mégoter	to skimp

*Il n'a pas **mégoté** sur les dépenses:* He didn't skimp on the expenses.

au diable l'avarice!	go on, spend and enjoy it! Who cares about the cost!

*«**Au diable l'avarice!**» a-t-il dit en commandant une troisième bouteille de champagne:* 'Let's spend and enjoy it!' he said, ordering a third bottle of champagne.

B

Bad/worthless

moche *
lousy, rotten (This is a much used word.)

*Selon le toubib il s'est fait un claquage. C'est vraiment **moche** ça, un jour avant le match:* According to the doc he has torn a muscle. That's really lousy, a day before the match.

dégueulasse *
filthy, awful

*Quel temps **dégueulasse**!:* What ghastly weather!

comme ci, comme ça
so-so

*Demain le temps sera **comme ci, comme ça**:* Tomorrow the weather will be so-so.

débile
pathetic, useless, feeble

ça ne casse rien
it's not up to much, it's no great shakes

*Ses premiers documentaires **n'ont rien cassé**:* His first documentaries were nothing to write home about.

pas fameux
not up to much, not too good

*Je vois que même dans le Midi le temps n'est **pas fameux** en ce moment:* I see that even in the south of France the weather is not up to much at the moment.

nul
useless, hopeless

*C'est **nul**, ce film:* This film is no good at all.

*Je suis **nul** en anglais:* I'm useless at English.

ça ne vaut pas un clou
it's no good at all, it's utterly worthless

le navet　　　　　　　　　　poor, inferior film

*Un **navet** si vous voulez mais je vous assure que ce film m'a rapporté gros:* A poor film if you like but I assure you it earned me a lot of money.

faire quelque chose par-　　to do something in a careless,
dessus la jambe　　　　　　casual way

c'est de la camelote　　　　it's junk, rubbish

le rossignol　　　　　　　　old junk, white elephant, vehicle
　　　　　　　　　　　　　　　which is hard to sell (normally
　　　　　　　　　　　　　　　'rossignol' = nightingale)

*J'ai expliqué à mon fils qu'il y a les bonnes motos et **les rossignols**:* I explained to my son that motorbikes come in two sorts – good ones and the ones you don't want to buy.

à la noix　　　　　　　　　feeble, pretty useless, crummy
à la godille
à la manque
à la mie de pain

*Un alibi **à la noix**:* A ropey alibi.

*Deux voleurs **à la mie de pain**:* Two mickey-mouse robbers.

en peau de lapin　　　　　　all sound (but doing nothing)

*Un gauchiste **en peau de lapin**:* A leftist on the surface only.

un roman de gare　　　　　a rather trashy novel (with the
　　　　　　　　　　　　　　　image of picking it up at the
　　　　　　　　　　　　　　　station bookstall just for passing
　　　　　　　　　　　　　　　the journey. The writer would be
　　　　　　　　　　　　　　　'un romancier/une romancière de
　　　　　　　　　　　　　　　gare'.)

ça craint!　　　　　　　　it's frightful, horrible

*Ta veste rouge et ta cravate verte, **ça craint!**:* Your red coat and your green tie – looks ghastly!

To go to Bed/sleep

faire dodo to go to sleep (from children's language)

au dodo 'bye-byes'

*On se remet **au dodo**:* We go back to sleep.

s'endormir comme une masse to go out like a light

roupiller to snooze

piquer un somme to have forty winks, a wee nap

une ronflette a snooze ('ronfler' = to snore)

*Après le déjeuner **une** petite **ronflette** vous fait du bien, selon ma femme:* A little snooze after lunch does you good according to my wife.

en écraser * to sleep like a log

se pieuter * to go to bed, hit the hay
se mettre au pieu *

les plumes (f) * bed
le plumard *

*«Mais à dix heures j'étais dans **les plumes»**, protesta-t-il au policier:* 'But at ten I was tucked up in bed', he protested to the policeman.

dans les bras de Morphée asleep (Morpheus was the Greek God of Dreams.)

*Je n'ai passé que quelques heures **dans les bras de Morphée**:* I only had a few hours' sleep.

une nuit blanche a sleepless night

*Je passe **une nuit blanche** et je me lève à six heures fatigué et de mauvaise humeur:* I hardly sleep and I get up at six feeling tired and in a bad mood.

To Beg

mendigoter * to beg ('mendier' in standard French)

faire la manche * to beg, to make a collection

Il chante un peu puis s'approche de nous pour faire la manche: He sings a bit then comes over to pass the hat round.

To Betray

donner quelqu'un to 'grass' on someone
vendre quelqu'un

balancer quelqu'un * to 'shop' someone

être brûlé to be 'blown'

Dès qu'un espion est brûlé, il faut qu'il disparaisse au plus vite: As soon as a spy's cover is blown he must disappear as quickly as possible.

vendre la mèche to let the cat out of the bag

Reste à savoir qui a vendu la mèche: It remains to be seen who gave the game away.

Blow/slap

la claque cuff, slap
la taloche
la baffe *

Il m'a collé une baffe: He clouted me one.

Body

la caboche * head, nut

la pince * hand

Je lui serre la pince: I shake hands.

Body

le pif *   nose

la guibole *   leg

le petit juif   funny bone

le bec   mouth

*La pipe **au bec***: With a pipe in his mouth.

la gueule   mouth (properly used of animals
                                      and impolitely and commonly
                                      used of people)

Ta gueule!: Shut up!

rouler les mécaniques *   to roll one's shoulders, to swagger

***Roulant les mécaniques**, il s'approche du bar*: He swaggers up to the
bar.

la feuille *   ear

*Être dur de **la feuille***: To be hard of hearing.

Boredom

mortel   deadly boring

*Je te préviens, ça va être **mortel**!*: I warn you, you'll be bored to death.

gluant   really boring

enquiquiner *   to bore

le métro-boulot-dodo   the boring routine of the
                                      commuter – train, work, sleep.
                                      For some it is the equally dreary
                                      'auto-boulot-dodo'.

Shaving is seen as particularly boring, hence the following (among others):

quelle barbe!   what a bore!

Quelle barbe! *Mes vacances vont me coûter encore plus cher!:* What a bore! My holidays are going to cost me even more!

rasoir   boring
rasant

barber   to bore

*Ça me **barbe** de l'écouter:* It's a bore listening to him.

une vieille barbe   a boring old person

C

To Carry

trimbaler   to cart around

*J'ai dû **trimbaler** tout ça:* I had to cart all that stuff around.

transbahuter *   to lug

Caution

au cas où   just in case

*Je prends ma lampe de poche **au cas où**:* I'm taking my torch just in case.

pas de vagues!   don't rock the boat! don't stir
                                    things up, don't make waves

filer doux   to lie low
se tenir peinard

*Depuis ce scandale il **file doux**:* Since this scandal he is keeping his head down.

Caution

y aller mollo * to adopt a softly softly approach, to tread carefully

*Tu vas voir le patron? Tu connais ses colères; il faut **y aller mollo**:* You are going to see the boss? You know how angry he gets; you'd better tread carefully.

Celebration

faire la noce to live it up
faire la bombe
faire la fête
faire la vie

arroser quelque chose to celebrate with a drink or two

*Il faut **arroser** ça!:* We must drink to that!

marquer le coup to mark the occasion

*Tu viens d'acheter cette décapotable? Il faut **marquer le coup**:* You have just bought this convertible? We must mark the event.

pavoiser to crow, to celebrate, to put out the flags

*Il n'y a pas lieu de **pavoiser**:* There's no call for rejoicing.

la troisième mi-temps post-match celebration (especially rugby), nineteenth hole (literally the third 'half' of the match)

*J'adore jouer au rugby mais je ne sais pas si ma femme approuve ces fameuses **troisièmes mi-temps**:* I love playing rugby but I'm not sure if my wife approves of these famous post-match get-togethers.

Certainty

c'est dans le sac it's in the bag
c'est dans la poche

c'est déja couru d'avance	it's a dead cert (like a race already run and won)
c'est du tout cuit *	it's a cinch (not to be confused with 'c'est cuit': it's all up)
craché (par terre), juré	I'll swear to it

Craché, juré, c'est un type vraiment généreux: I swear to it, he's a really generous chap.

Change

| virer sa cuti | to change one's lifestyle, to break out into a new life |

Character/ attitude

| la lavette
la poule mouillée | drip, sop, a pretty good wimp |
| le béni-oui-oui
dire amen à tout | yes-man |

*Ils avaient peur de lui et **disaient amen à tout***: They were afraid of him and went along with every proposal.

| froussard | frightened, chicken |
| cabochard | stubborn |

*Je suppose que je suis un peu **cabochard** de nature*: I suppose by nature I like digging my heels in a bit.

cachottier	secretive
gonflé à bloc	full of pep, psyched up
ramenard *	loud-mouthed
ne douter de rien	to be full of self-confidence, to be ready to take on anything, not be backward in coming forward

Character/attitude

cocorico patriotic (to France)

*Je suis **cocorico**. Je roule en Renault:* I'm patriotic, I drive a Renault.

dans le vent with it

*Il se veut **dans le vent**:* He tries to be trendy.

*C'est normal, la plupart des élèves préfèrent un prof qui est jeune et **dans le vent**:* It's only natural, most pupils prefer a teacher who is young and with it.

branché switched on, trendy
câblé
chébran * 'chébran' is an example of 'le verlan' (a kind of back slang), in this case of 'branché'. There has been a renewed interest in 'le verlan' recently.

*Déçus, nous avons décidé d'essayer de trouver une boîte plus **branchée**:* We were disappointed, so we decided to try and find a more trendy nightclub.

ringard 'square'
mimile *
beauf *

*Je porte toujours mon jean délavé pour éviter d'être **mimile**:* I aways wear my faded jeans so as to seem with it.

*Cela se vend bien, même chez les jeunes, malgré son image un peu **ringarde**:* It sells well, even among the young, in spite of its rather dated image.

avoir bouffé du lion to be full of drive, to be up and 'at 'em'

*Attention! Le président **a bouffé du lion**!:* Watch out! The chairman is rushing around, full of go!

c'est une fine mouche there are no flies on him

le charlot   'comedian'

Nous avons perdu beaucoup de matches mais nous ne sommes pas des charlots: We've lost a lot of matches but we are serious players.

peinard   without a worry, jogging along nicely

le père peinard   calm, unhurried sort of chap

une Marie-Chantal   a snobbish, hoity-toity person (The expression can also be used of a man.)

Je ne suis pas une Marie-Chantal. J'aime la musique pop aussi!: I'm not a highbrow snob. I like pop music as well!

être dessalé   to be street-wise, to have one's eyes open

être dégourdi   to be sharp, to know it all

parano   paranoid (from 'paranoïaque')

Après cet accident quelques touristes paranos ont refusé de voyager: After this accident some tourists, full of unreasonable fear, refused to travel.

rosse   nasty, bitchy

un ours mal léché   a boor

mal dégrossi   rough, boorish

le baroudeur   fighter, scrapper

C'est un baroudeur

Character/attitude

ne pas faire le détail to go wholeheartedly and successfully at something without worrying about the finer points

la locomotive leader, trend-setter

*Champion pour la troisième fois, c'est lui **la locomotive** qui va motiver nos joueurs:* Champion for the third time, he's the one who will pull along and motivate all our players.

ne pas faire de chichis not to make a fuss

*Je n'ai **pas fait de chichis** et j'ai dit oui bien que je n'aime pas travailler le samedi:* I didn't make a fuss and I said yes though I don't like working Saturdays.

être pantouflard to be stay-at-home (for a man, with the image of carpet slippers and a seat by the fire)

être pot-au-feu to be stay-at-home (for a woman, with the image of the kitchen and pots and pans)

la vie à cent à l'heure life in the fast lane (even though the limit is in fact 130 km/h)

Cheap

c'est donné it's a gift, a snip, really cheap

*Quatre mille francs! Ce n'est pas **donné**!:* Four thousand francs! It's not cheap!

pour une bouchée de pain for a song

*Je l'ai eu **pour une bouchée de pain**:* I paid hardly anything for it.

pour trois fois rien for next to nothing

Petites Révisions – Test Yourself!

PETITES REVISIONS 1
(Abandonment – Cheap)

Translations page 173

1. Elle a traversé le désert toute seule. Ce n'est pas rien!
2. Au lieu de tout plaquer, tu as travaillé dur et tu es devenu millionnaire. Chapeau!
3. On fait une balade dimanche? Ça colle?
4. Je vais lire un bon polar avec personne ici pour me casser les pieds.
5. Le toubib m'a dit de rester au lit. C'est moche ça.
6. Allez! Onze heures. On va faire dodo. D'ac?
7. Demain lundi – et on reprend le métro-boulot-dodo.
8. Je ne veux pas voir ses diapos. Ça va être mortel!
9. On va dans une boîte. On va se marrer.
10. Achetez-le! C'est donné.

Children

le galopin	young rascal
le (la) gamin(e)	youngster
le (la) gosse	kid

*Au loin un **gosse** tapait dans un ballon:* In the distance a kid was kicking a ball around.

le lardon *	brat
le (la) môme	kid, boy, girl
le morveux *	brat (the adjective 'morveux' = snotty-nosed)
la marmaille *	kids, brood
un petit bout de chou	a sweet little thing
le petit monstre	child, little horror (humorous), holy terror

*Merci de garder Jean-Pierre ce soir, mais je te préviens, c'est un vrai **petit monstre**!:* Thanks for babysitting tonight, but I warn you, Jean-Pierre is a right little horror!

les chères têtes blondes	dear little ones (ironical)

*Quand je suis rentré **les chères têtes blondes** avaient vidé toutes les bouteilles:* When I got home the dear little ones had emptied all the bottles.

Choice

la balle est dans votre camp/the ball is in your court
dans le camp de

*La balle est maintenant **dans le camp de**s professeurs:* The ball is now in the teachers' court.

Cigarettes/smoking

la sèche   fag

*File-moi **une sèche**, mon vieux:* Slip me a fag, old chap.

la cibiche *   cig, fag
la clope *

le mégot   cigarette end

*Le gamin a écrasé son **mégot** en me voyant:* The youngster stubbed out
his cigarette on seeing me.

en griller une *   to have a drag

la bouffarde   pipe

*Il tire sur sa **bouffarde**:* He puffs at his pipe.

Clarity

faire un dessin/croquis   to spell it out, to make oneself
                                        clear

*Bon, bon, j'ai compris. Pas besoin de me **faire un dessin**:* OK, OK,
I've got the picture, no need to spell it out to me.

c'est net et sans bavure!   it's absolutely clear!

j'te dis pas   I don't have to tell you
j'te raconte pas   (you can just imagine)

*C'est pas facile. **J'te dis pas**:* It's not easy. I don't have to tell you.

c'est la bouteille à l'encre   it's as clear as mud, a proper
                                        muddle, you can't tell what's what

en bon français   in plain English

Clothes

s'habiller au décrochez-moi-ça

to dress cheaply, in old 'bargain' clothes (from 'décrocher' = to take off the peg)

les fringues (f) *

clothes

*La vue de Jean-Paul serré dans un jean troué me fait sourire. Il se fiche de ses **fringues**:* The sight of Jean-Paul wearing tight holed jeans makes me smile. He doesn't care what he wears.

les nippes (f)

togs

le costard *

suit (can have something of the pinstripe image)

*Tu aurais dû me voir dans mon **costard**-cravate:* You should have seen me in my suit and tie.

le falzar *
le froc *

trousers

les pattes d'eph (f)

trousers with large bell-bottoms (from 'pattes d'éléphant')

*A la mode ou pas, André adore ses **pattes d'eph**:* Fashionable or not, André loves his bell-bottoms.

les godasses (f)

shoes, boots

*Je lace mes **godasses** en sortant de la banque et je vois le flic qui me regarde:* I do up my shoes when I come out of the bank and I see the copper looking at me.

le pull

pullover, sweater (from 'le pullover')

la petite laine

winter woolly

*Il commence à faire froid. On supporte une **petite laine**:* It's beginning to get cold. One could do with a sweater

l'imper (m)

mac (from 'imperméable')

L'imper

le sweat   sweatshirt (a typical French
                                abbreviation)

le melon   bowler hat (from 'le chapeau
                                melon')

le survêt   tracksuit (from 'le survêtement de
                                sport')

De nos jours, si on met son **survêt**, *cela ne veut pas forcément dire
qu'on va faire du jogging:* Nowadays, if you put on your tracksuit, that
doesn't necessarily mean you are going jogging.

le pap *   bow-tie (from 'le nœud papillon',
                                a reference to the butterfly shape)

Le pap

le smok *   D.J., dinner jacket (from 'le
                                smoking')

la liquette *   shirt

la queue de pie   tails

les tennis (m)   tennis, gym shoes

Il s'approche silencieusement dans ses **tennis**: He comes up silently in
his gym shoes.

Clothes

les baskets (m)	trainers
tomber la veste	to shed one's jacket
se saper *	to dress
être sapé	

*Un type **sapé** tout en noir:* A chap got up all in black.

s'attifer	to tog oneself up
être fagoté comme l'as de pique *	to look a sight

To feel Cold

être frigorifié	to be frozen

*Un public **frigorifié**:* An audience chilled to the bone.

cailler *	to be freezing
peler *	

*Le chauffage ne marche pas. Je **caille**!:* The heating is not working. I'm absolutely freezing!

Collusion

être en cheville avec quelqu'un	to be in league, in cahoots with someone
être de mèche *	

*Peut-être que ces contrebandiers travaillent **en cheville avec** les pêcheurs?:* Perhaps these smugglers are working together with the fishermen?

Competition/ rivalry

faire la pige à quelqu'un *   to outdo someone, knock spots off someone

*Il boit bière sur bière. Il **fait la pige à** tous ses amis:* He knocks back beer after beer. His friends can't compete.

se tirer la bourre   to compete

*Ces pizzérias **se tirent la bourre** à tout-va:* These pizza restaurants have a ding-dong rivalry.

Confession

se mettre à table *   to spill the beans, cough up
manger le morceau *

*On lui a parlé gentiment et **il s'est mis à table** tout de suite:* We spoke nicely to him and he coughed up at once.

Confidentiality

entre quatre-z-yeux   privately, between you, me and the gatepost

*C'est ce qu'on se dit **entre quatre-z-yeux**:* It's what is being said privately.

motus!   keep it under your hat! not a
bouche cousue!   word to a soul!

*Jusqu'ici le voleur demeure **bouche cousue**:* So far the thief hasn't said a single word.

motus et bouche cousue!   (The two expressions are often used together.)

Control

perdre les pédales *   to lose one's head, to lose control
(It is not surprising that cycling
should provide a number of
expressions such as this one, just
as in English some come from
cricket: to be on a sticky wicket,
for example.)

*Du calme! Si vous **perdez les pédales** maintenant, c'est fini!:* Keep
calm! If you loose your grip now, it's all over.

Courage

avoir du cran   to have guts, plenty of pluck
**avoir le cœur bien
accroché**
avoir du cœur au ventre

être gonflé   to be brave, to have plenty of
nerve

le courage arrosé   Dutch courage (courage helped by
alcohol, see 'arroser' under
Celebration)

tenir le coup   to hold out, last out, stick it out

avoir du sang de navet   to be a timorous type ('navet' =
turnip)

**ne pas avoir froid aux
yeux**   to be plucky

*Mais cette fois le voyou tombe sur une caissière qui n'a **pas froid aux
yeux**:* But this time the yobbo comes across a cashier who is not going to
be frightened.

Crime/criminals/illegality

le milieu	underworld, criminal fraternity
le filou	clever thief, swindler
le blouson noir	hooligan (a reference to the black leather jacket)
le blouson doré	hooligan from a rich family, Yuppie yob
le loubard	hooligan, young yob
la (petite) frappe **le malfrat**	hooligan, thug

*Les **malfrats** du quartier font peur aux touristes:* The local thugs frighten the tourists.

le truand	gangster

*Pourtant ce **truand** au revolver facile n'oppose aucune résistance:* However, this gangster, quick to use a gun, offers no resistance.

le demi-sel	second-league crook (who is not as tough as he thinks)
le J.V.	hooligan (from 'le jeune voyou'), juvenile delinquent

*Trois **J.V.** ont menacé le facteur:* Three hooligans threatened the postman.

le caïd *	big boss (crime), Mister Big
braquer *	to hold up

*C'est lui qui a **braqué** la banque:* He's the one who held up the bank.

l'arnaque (f) *	con trick, 'sting'

Crime/criminals/illegality

le monte-en-l'air   cat burglar

Un **monte-en-l'air** qui se respecte n'aurait jamais fait tant de bruit: A self-respecting cat burglar would never have made so much noise.

le vol à la roulotte   stealing things from parked cars

le corbeau   poison-pen letter writer (normally 'corbeau' = crow)

Les rumeurs vont bon train. Qui est **le corbeau**? C'est elle? Ou lui? Ou vous?: Rumours are rife. Who is the poison-pen letter writer? She could be the one. Or he could. Or you?

le fric-frac *   break-in, 'job'
le casse *

descendre quelqu'un   to kill, 'bump off' someone
faire la peau à quelqu'un

On a dû **le descendre** au moment où il ouvrait la portière: He must have been shot just as he was opening the car door.

planter *   to stab

Ne bouge pas ou je te **plante**: Don't move or I'll stick this into you.

le pot de vin   bribe, under-the-counter payment
le dessous de table

S'il touche des **pots de vin**, c'est bien sérieux: If he's taking bribes, it's a serious matter.

graisser la patte à   to bribe someone, to slip
quelqu'un   someone something

le toxico   drug addict, junky (from
le camé *   'toxicomane')

Un **camé** à douze ans: A junky at twelve.

le chèque en bois	dud cheque
la combine	fiddling, double dealing, wangle
la cuisine	'cooking' (of the books), dubious scheming
carotter	to fiddle, wangle
faucher	to pinch, nick (There are many
piquer	words for 'to steal'. 'Faucher' and
chiper	'piquer' are very common.)

*Il l'a **fauché** dans un supermarché*: He nicked it from a supermarket.

*Ils ont **piqué** une bagnole pour faire un tour avec*: They pinched a car to go for a joyride.

barboter	to swipe, filch, lift, steal
chaparder	
subtiliser	
souffler	

*Il s'est fait **subtiliser** son porte-feuille par un gosse*: Some kid whipped his wallet.

*Il s'est fait **souffler** le premier prix par son cousin*: His cousin snatched the first prize from him.

To Cry

y aller de sa petite larme	to have a bit of a cry
chialer *	to cry, blub

*Des coups de déveine à en **chialer**: Strokes of bad luck to make you weep.

D

To Deceive/swindle

mettre quelqu'un dedans	to take in, to diddle someone

To Deceive/swindle

se faire avoir/rouler — to be 'had', conned

rouler quelqu'un (dans la farine) — to 'do' someone, to take someone for a ride

mener quelqu'un en bateau — to string someone along, to lead someone up the garden path

*C'est drôle mais j'ai l'impression que ce jeune homme charmant veut me **mener en bateau**:* It's odd but I get the feeling that this charming young man is trying to take me for a ride.

posséder quelqu'un — to fool, dupe someone

*Cette fois ils nous ont **possédés**, c'est vrai:* This time they diddled us, it's true.

blouser quelqu'un * — to swindle, trick someone

matraquer — to clobber

*Il ne s'agit pas de **matraquer** nos clients:* It's not a question of clobbering our customers.

le bobard — untruth, tall story

le boniment — smooth talk

*Assez de **boniment**!:* Enough of your smooth talk!

avoir la berlue — not to be seeing straight

*Est-ce que j'ai **eu la berlue**? Mais non, le mot «danger» était bien là:* Had I been seeing things? No, the word 'danger' was there all right.

n'y voir que du bleu — to be bamboozled, not to catch on

être marron */chocolat * — to be caught out, to be 'had'

*Me voilà **chocolat**!:* I've been done!

faut pas me la faire! * — now then, don't try that on me!

*Je lui ai expliqué que j'étais du métier et qu'il ne **fallait pas me la faire**:* I explained to him I was in the business and it was no good trying it on me.

Demonstration

la manif   political demo (from 'manifestation')

*Dix blessés dans une **manif** hier:* Ten hurt in a demo yesterday.

Depression

la déprime   (fit of) depression

*J'ai peur qu'elle ne sombre dans **la déprime**:* I am afraid she may sink into depression.

avoir le cafard **broyer du noir**	to have the blues, to be down in the dumps ('cafard' = cockroach)
être dans le trente-sixième dessous	to be at a very low ebb
avoir le moral dans les chaussettes	to be really down, to feel very low

To Deserve

il ne l'a pas volé **il l'a cherché**	he asked for it, he had it coming to him

*Si on le met à la porte, **il ne l'aura pas volé**:* If he is kicked out, it'll serve him right.

This expression is sometimes used in a positive sense:

*Un poste excellent. **Il ne l'a pas volé**:* An excellent job. He deserved it.

ça te fera les pieds *   it'll serve you right

To Deserve

être pain bénit
to serve one right, to get one's just deserts

être servi
to get one's fill, to get it and how

*Quel film! Les amateurs de grands frissons vont **être servis**!*: What a film! Those who like thrills and shivers will get all they want!

To Die

crever
to die, peg out (a very common word)

casser sa pipe *
passer l'arme à gauche *
to kick the bucket

y passer
y rester
y laisser sa peau
to lose one's life

*J'ai failli **y rester***: I was nearly a dead man.

*Il a failli **y passer***: He nearly 'bought' it.

Difference

c'est une autre paire de manches
it's a different kettle of fish

c'est une autre chanson
that's a different story, it's a different ball game

*Côté argent, **c'est une autre chanson***: Moneywise, it's a different story.

il y a un monde entre ...
there's a world of difference between ...

Entre** critique et réprimande **il y a un monde: There's a world of difference between criticism and reproof.

Difficulty/problem

le hic snag

*Je suis dans le rouge. C'est là **le hic**!:* I am in the red. That's the snag!

l'anicroche (f) hitch

*On espère que tout se passera cette fois sans **anicroche**:* We hope that everything will go off without a hitch this time.

le pépin hitch, problem

*Un **pépin** de dernière minute:* a last minute hitch.

*Un **pépin** de santé:* A bit of a health problem.

il y a un os * there's a difficulty, problem

il y a de l'eau dans le gaz there's something amiss, there's something not quite right

il y a quelque chose qui cloche there's something wrong

c'est coton * it's tough, very difficult

*Ça va être **coton** d'en trouver:* It'll be hard-going to find some.

dur, dur hard, far from easy

*J'ai repris le boulot ce matin après un weekend au bord de la mer; **dur, dur**:* I went back to work this morning after a weekend by the sea. Hard-going!

ce n'est pas de la tarte * it's no easy job

*Dormir par un temps pareil, **ce n'est pas de la tarte**:* It's not easy to sleep in weather like this.

c'est la croix et la bannière it's a hell of a job

***C'est la croix et la bannière** pour faire manger ce gosse:* It's a hell of a job to get this kid to eat.

Difficulty/problem

en baver *   to suffer

*Tu as corrigé tout ça en une heure? Tu as dû **en baver**:* You corrected all that in an hour? It must have been a hell of a sweat for you.

ce n'est pas évident   it's not easy (to see how it's done)

*Il doit répondre à toutes ces lettres. **Ce n'est pas évident**:* He has to answer all these letters. No easy task.

il n'y a pas moyen de   (there's) no way (it can be done)
moyenner
il n'y a pas mèche *

ne pas être de tout repos   not to be easy, plain sailing, certain

*Mon rôle ne sera pas **de tout repos**:* My job won't be plain sailing.

tomber sur un bec   to hit a snag, run into a difficulty, run into trouble ('le bec' refers to 'le bec de gaz' = lamppost)

se casser le nez   to come unstuck

pédaler dans la   to get bogged down (with the
choucroute *   nightmarish image of pedalling hard and getting nowhere)

ne pas faire avancer le   not to get one anywhere
schmilblic *

*C'est un drôle de jugement qui ne **fait** guère **avancer le schmilblic**:* It's an odd judgement which doesn't get us much further on.

être coincé   to be in a fix, stuck

*Financièrement, vous n'êtes pas le seul à **être coincé** en ce moment:* You are not the only one to be in a tricky financial position at the moment.

être dans de jolis draps   to be in a fix, a fine situation

être dans le pétrin
le pastis *
la mélasse
to be in the soup

*Tu vois dans quel **pétrin** je suis:* You see what a spot I'm in.

*Pour comble de **pastis** ...:* To crown it all ...

donner du fil à retordre
à quelqu'un
to give someone problems (of people and things)

*Traduire cent pages en une semaine, ça m'a **donné du fil à retordre**:* It was a real job to translate a hundred pages in a week.

c'est une vraie galère
this is hell, it's utter hell (from 'galère' = galley/convict ship)

*Mais qu'est-ce qu'il allait faire dans cette **galère**?:* But what on earth was he doing letting himself in for this?

ne pas être sorti de
l'auberge
not to be out of the woods

*Il m'a parlé sévèrement et m'a dit que je **n'étais pas** encore **sorti de l'auberge**:* He spoke to me severely and said that I wasn't yet out of the woods.

à quelle sauce va-t-on être
mangé?
what is going to befall us?

avoir les yeux plus grands
que le ventre
to bite off more than one can chew

ce n'est pas un cadeau
it's no push over

*Diriger un journal, **ce n'est pas un cadeau**:* Running a newspaper isn't just an easy job.

ce n'est pas une partie de
plaisir
it's no picnic

*L'atterrissage par mauvais temps **n'est pas une partie de plaisir**:* Landing in bad weather is no picnic.

il n'y a pas trente-six
solutions
there's only one solution

Difficulty/problem

être au bout de son rouleau — to be at the end of one's tether

la colle — tricky question

*Vous me posez une **colle**!*: You've got me there! Ask me another!

ça ne tourne pas rond — things aren't going too well

*Si **ça ne tourne pas rond**, dites-le au patron:* If there's a problem, tell the boss.

tout va très bien, Madame la Marquise — I assure you all is well (The inference is that it is not. The words come from a well-known song. When Madame rings up for news, her staff assure her that all is well … 'except' for the mare dying … in a fire in the stable … when the chateau caught fire, when her husband, finding he was ruined, committed suicide and upset all the candles.)

*Le public s'inquiète, mais c'est toujours le même «**tout va très bien, Madame la Marquise**»:* The public is concerned but it's always the same 'all's well, don't worry'.

Direction/distance/locality

tous azimuts — from all sides, in all directions, here, there and everywhere

*J'ai téléphoné **tous azimuts** pour trouver une chambre:* I telephoned high and low to find a room.

cap sur — off to (from 'mettre le cap sur' = to head for, of nautical origin)

***Cap sur** le Midi ensoleillé!*: Off to the sunny South!

Cap sur *le casino!:* Off to the casino!

ça fait une trotte   it's quite a way

la borne   kilometre (a standard meaning of 'borne' = milestone)

Nous avons encore trois cents **bornes** *à parcourir:* We've another three hundred kilometres to go.

pousser une pointe   to push on

On pourra **pousser une pointe** *jusqu'à Nice:* We'll be able to push on to Nice.

dans le secteur   in the region, roundabout

Je me demande pourquoi il y a tant de gendarmes **dans le secteur**: I wonder why there are so many policemen around the place.

être du coin   to be from around here

*Le camionneur m'a demandé si j'***étais du coin**: The lorry driver asked me if I was local.

dans les parages   in the vicinity (of nautical origin)

le bled *   village, town, dump (of Arabic origin)

le patelin   place, dump

Je sors pour faire le tour du **patelin**: I go out to have a look around.

un petit trou   a hole, a small place

Un petit trou *perdu:* A godforsaken hole.

Un petit trou *pas cher:* A cheap, modest little place, resort.

la cambrousse *   countryside

Il va faire drôlement beau et j'ai envie d'aller jouir des plaisirs de **la cambrousse**: It is going to be really good weather and I feel like enjoying the pleasures of the countryside.

au diable vauvert   miles from anywhere, stuck out in the countryside

Disappointment

la douche écossaise ups and downs (of feelings, hopes) (The image is of the alternating hot and cold water of a shower.)

Demain **la douche écossaise** *– le soleil ne brillera plus et il fera froid:* Tomorrow we're in for a nasty change – no sunshine and it'll be cold.

To Dismiss/throw out

sacquer quelqu'un to sack someone

virer quelqu'un to throw out, to give someone the
vider order of the boot

flanquer quelqu'un à la to chuck, fling someone out, to
porte get rid of someone

limoger quelqu'un to sack, dismiss someone (Officers used to be 'retired' to Limoges. It is interesting to note that we send people to Coventry with a meaning which is not too dissimilar, and that both cities are more or less centrally situated.)

mettre au rencart to chuck out, get rid of (people and things)

Des fonctionnaires **mis au rencart***:* Officials who have been put out to grass.

jeter quelque chose aux to throw out, chuck overboard
orties * ('l'ortie' = nettle)

Quant à la discipline, il l'a **jetée aux orties***. Tant pis si les élèves trichent:* As for discipline, he has chucked it out of the window. Too bad if pupils cheat.

Dog

le toutou dog, doggie (from children's language)

France too likes clean pavements and doggies to use the gutter instead – hence this publicity slogan:

*N'oubliez pas d'apprendre le caniveau à votre **toutou**:* Don't forget to teach your doggie how to use the gutter. (Don't let it foul the pavement.)

Le toutou

le chienchien dear little doggie

*J'aime voir les vieilles dames élégantes qui promènent leurs **chienchiens** quel que soit le temps:* I like seeing the elegant old ladies walking their doggies whatever the weather.

le cabot * dog, hound, pooch
le clebs *

Door

la lourde * door

*Boucle **la lourde**!:* Shut the door!

Drink

le pinard wine, vino, plonk

Drink

Le pinard

le Château-la-Pompe **la flotte**	water (a mocking comparison with 'château' wines)
l'apéro (m)	aperitif

*L'heure de **l'apéro**:* The happy hour.

Le gros rouge (qui tache)	red plonk
le pousse-café	liqueur (taken with coffee after a meal)
le pousse-au-crime *	fiery spirits
le calva	calvados (cider brandy from Normandy)

*J'ai pris un café-**calva**:* I had a coffee and calvados.

le trou normand	the glass of strong calvados taken between courses to help the digestion and traditionally drunk in one go
boire sur le zinc	to drink at the bar (a reference to the material of the café counter. You can expect a lower price at the 'comptoir' than if you sit in the 'salle' or on the 'terrasse'.)

le bouillon d'onze heures   (drink of) poison (certainly not to
be confused with English
'elevenses' in any form!)

le pot *   drink, jar

*Un **pot** d'adieu:* A farewell drink.

le galopin *   small beer, 'half'

*Je ne bois pas beaucoup, à la rigueur un **galopin** à une terrasse avec
quelques amis:* I don't drink much, if pushed, a small beer on a café
terrace with some friends.

le ballon   'balloon' glass

*Un **ballon** de rouge:* A glass of red.

le cadavre   empty bottle, 'dead man'
(normally 'cadavre' = corpse)

elle est morte   that one's finished, another dead
'un (bottle)

le coup de l'étrier   one for the road (literally 'stirrup-
cup')

boire un coup   to have a drink

The French have a popular song starting with these words:

***Boire un** petit **coup** c'est agréable:* It's nice to have a little drink.

boire sec   to knock it back, to be a hard
drinker

faire cul sec   to down it in one

*Malheureusement il m'a persuadé de **faire cul sec**:* Unfortunately he
persuaded me to down it at one go.

siffler   to down (a drink), to sink
descendre

être en goguette   to be out boozing, carousing
être en ribote

Drink

s'en jeter un (derrière la la cravate) *	to have a drink, knock one back
picoler	to drink (a lot), to booze
se rincer la dalle *	to wet one's whistle
il carbure au whisky	whisky is his tipple, poison, his usual drink
boire à tire-larigot	to drink like a fish
tuer le ver	to have a hair of the dog that bit one (a drop of the hard stuff in the morning, on an empty stomach, to cure, hopefully, hangover effects)
c'est un pilier de bar il est toujours pendu au bar	he's always propping up the bar
à la bonne vôtre à la tienne! à vos amours!	cheers! here's to you!
à la tienne Etienne! *	here's mud in your eye! (There are one or two rhyming expressions of this sort reminiscent of our once popular 'see yer later, alligator!')

Drunk

noir	drunk, plastered
gris	tipsy
paf * **bourré *** **rond ***	drunk, sloshed

*Ils sont rentrés un peu **pafs** et Charles a mis cinq minutes pour trouver sa clé:* They came home a bit drunk and Charles took five minutes to find his key.

avoir un verre dans le nez	to have had a few
prendre une cuite */ **biture** *	to get sloshed
avoir fait le plein	to have got tanked up
plein comme un œuf *	to have had a skinful, to be well away
avoir mal aux cheveux **avoir la GDB** *	to have a hangover (from 'la gueule de bois')
cuver son vin	to sleep it off
l'alcoolo (m)	alcoholic, heavy drinker

Il s'en jette un derrière la cravate

E

Ease/contentment

être bien dans sa peau	to feel at ease, happy
être à l'aise dans ses baskets *	to feel at ease, relaxed ('les baskets' = basket-ball shoes, so the image is one of cool relaxation in trainers and jeans)

*Malgré tous ses soucis, il a toujours l'air d'**être à l'aise dans ses baskets**: In spite of all his worries, he still looks thoroughly at ease.*

Ease/contentment

être tranquille comme Baptiste

to feel quite unconcerned, unruffled

être sur un petit nuage rose

to feel very happy, to be on cloud nine, to be in another world

*Elle **est sur un petit nuage rose**; on vient de libérer son mari:* She is on a high; her husband has just been freed.

tout baigne (dans l'huile) *
ça baigne! *

all is fine, super-duper (Whether it is cooking oil or engine oil, it all helps things to run nice and smoothly.)

*Ils ont gagné le gros lot et **ça baigne**!:* They've won the pools and everything is marvellous!

boire du petit lait

to lap it up, to enjoy every word (of praise), to feel pleased with oneself

Ease/facility

ça marche comme sur des roulettes

it is all going smoothly, it works like a charm ('roulettes' = castors)

ça passe comme une lettre à la poste

it's easy as anything, it couldn't be simpler

c'est simple comme bonjour

it's dead easy

*Alors on actionne quelques boutons et ça y est. **C'est simple comme bonjour**:* Then you twiddle a few knobs and there you are. Dead easy.

ce n'est pas bien sorcier

it's easy, there's really nothing to it

ce n'est pas la mer à boire	it's no great problem, it's not that hard
c'est du gâteau	it's a piece of cake
les doigts dans le nez *	easily, effortlessly
(comme) dans un fauteuil	easily

Il est arrivé **comme dans un fauteuil**: He cantered home.

comme un rien	with no problem

Formidable! Il remet les plombs **comme un rien**: Terrific! He changes the fuses just like that.

la promenade	walk-over, doddle, push-over
la balade	

Ce rallye n'est pas une **promenade**: This rally is no doddle.

Notre devoir de Maths, c'est **la balade**: Our Maths prep/homework is a doddle.

comme une fleur	easily, smoothly

Il arrive **comme une fleur**: He just strolls in.

Petites Révisions - Test Yourself!

PETITES REVISIONS 2
(Children – Ease/facility)

Translations page 173

1 «T'as une sèche?» me demande le môme.
2 N'oublie pas ta petite laine et ton imper.
3 Je caille ici! Je bois un calva pour me réchauffer.
4 On a le temps de s'en jeter un derrière la cravate.
5 Il a pris une cuite et ce matin il a mal aux cheveux.
6 Pas de problème, c'est du gâteau!
7 Je l'admire; il a fait ça les doigts dans le nez.
8 On prend un pot avant d'aller à la manif.
9 Trouver les objets perdus, ça ne va pas être de la tarte. C'est là le hic.
10 Je crois qu'il essaie de me mener en bateau. En attendant, motus et bouche cousue!

Effort

(il faut que) ça passe　　　　　(it's) make or break, all or nothing
ou ça casse

*Tu me connais. Quand j'entreprends quelque chose, c'est jusqu'au bout. C'est dans ma nature. Il n'y a pas de demi-mesures. **Ça passe ou ça casse**:* You know me. When I undertake something, I see it through. I am like that. There are no half-measures. All or nothing.

ne pas faire dans la dentelle not to pull any punches, to go
　　　　　　　　　　　　　　　　straight in ('la dentelle' = lace)

*Tout cela va changer avec un nouveau chef. C'est un homme dynamique qui **ne fait pas dans la dentelle**:* All that is going to change with a new leader. He's a dynamic man who goes straight in.

en mettre un coup	to make a big effort, to put something into it
se secouer	to snap out of it, to stir oneself, to pull one's socks up
mettre la gomme * **mettre le paquet** *	to pull out all the stops

*Face à cette violence, le gouvernement doit **mettre le paquet** pour protéger le public:* Faced with this violence the government must go flat out to protect the public.

se donner un mal de chien **pour faire quelque chose** **se plier en quatre**	to go to great trouble, to lean over backwards to do something
se décarcasser pour faire **quelque chose** *	to sweat one's guts out to do something
se saigner aux quatre veines	to make great sacrifices

*Elle **s'est saignée aux quatre veines** pour que ses enfants aient un peu d'argent:* She made great sacrifices so that her children should have a little money.

mettre les bouchées　　　to get cracking
doubles

*J'avais presque oublié la date limite. Il faut que je **mette les
bouchées doubles**:* I had almost forgotten the deadline. I must get
cracking.

se casser la tête　　　to rack one's brains
se triturer les méninges *

Embarrassment

être gêné aux　　　to feel embarrassed
entournures　　　('entournures' = armholes and the
　　　　　　　　　　　image is of ill-fitting ones)

*Nous sommes un peu **gênés aux entournures** d'apprendre que le
port de la veste est de rigueur:* We are a bit embarrassed to learn that a
jacket must be worn.

être dans ses petits souliers　to feel uncomfortable (as one
　　　　　　　　　　　　　would with shoes too small)

*J'**étais dans mes petits souliers** à l'idée d'aller voir son père:* I felt
awkward at the idea of going to see her father.

Enthusiasm

emballer　　　to enthuse, to excite
s'emballer　　　to get carried away

*Mes enfants sont plutôt sportifs. La lecture ne les **emballe** pas:* My
children prefer sport on the whole. They are not wild about reading.

être chaud　　　to be keen
être chaud chaud　　　(more familiar)

*Ils ne **sont** pas **chauds** pour attaquer tout de suite:* They aren't keen
on attacking straight away.

Enthusiasm

être partant to be on, a starter

T'es partant?: Are you game? Can I count you in?

être accro to be hooked, to be into something (from 'accroché' and drug language)

*Les **accros** de mode:* Fashion freaks.

le virus bug, enthusiasm, passion

*Il a deux **virus** – le théâtre et le cinéma:* He has two passions – the theatre and the cinema.

être tout feu tout flamme to be very keen, full of starry-eyed enthusiasm

brancher to turn on

*Malheureusement il y a peu de films de ce genre qui me **branchent**:* Unfortunately there are few films of this kind which really interest me.

on ne se bouscule pas au portillon there's no wild rush (The basic image is of people jostling at the barrier to get onto the platform for the underground.)

Ça se bouscule au portillon

*Le poste est maintenant vacant, mais **on ne se bouscule pas au portillon**:* The job is going, but there's no great rush for it.

le mordu   enthusiast (from 'mordre' = to bite)

*Etre un **mordu** de ski:* To be ski-mad.

le fana *   fan (from 'fanatique')

un enragé   someone who is wild about something, very keen on something

ça ne me dit rien   I'm not keen on the idea, it
ça ne me chante pas   doesn't appeal to me
ça ne me sourit pas

Evasion

se défiler   to shirk, get out of something

*Son père m'a demandé de le faire et je ne peux pas **me défiler**:* His father asked me and I can't get out of it.

Exaggeration

c'est un peu fort de café   that's going a bit far, pushing it a bit, a bit over the top

forcer la dose   to go too far, to push too hard

en remettre   to lay it on
en rajouter
ne pas y aller avec le dos
de la cuillère

*Il aime toujours **en rajouter** un peu:* He always likes to lay it on a bit.

le baratin   smooth talk, sales talk, glib talk

Exaggeration

(faire de) la pub
faire du battage

to plug, push, hype ('pub' from 'publicité')

*Sans **pub** on ne vend rien, paraît-il:* You've got to push things or you don't sell anything, it seems.

Excellence

au poil   super, smashing

à tout casser   smashing, slap-up

*Un dîner **à tout casser**:* A slap-up dinner.

extra   super, great, extra special

*Un petit restau **extra**:* A really good little restaurant.

*Des voisins **extras**:* Super neighbours.

sensas   fantastic (from 'sensationnel')

formid   terrific (from 'formidable')

impec   perfect (from 'impeccable')

chouette   terrific, super

dément   great, brill (normally 'dément' = mad)

chic alors!   great!

c'est le pied! */le super pied! *   fantastic!

*Ce n'était pas **le super-pied** mais c'était pas mal:* It wasn't super-duper but it wasn't bad.

génial   brilliant

*T'as vu ce film d'épouvante hier soir? **Génial**!*: Did you see that horror film last night? Brilliant!

pas dégueu! *	not bad! i.e., pretty good! (from 'dégueulasse')
terrible *	terrific (Note that the familiar meaning is the exact opposite of the normal one. Such a device makes the word very vivid. Compare words like 'mean' and 'wicked' in current English slang.)

*Des cocktails **terribles**:* Really super cocktails.

*Ça ne va pas **terrible** en ce moment:* Things aren't too good at the moment.

du tonnerre, de tous les tonnerres	terrific

*Un film **de tous les tonnerres**:* A FANtastic film!

hénaurme	tremendous (from 'énorme')

*Un acteur **hénaurme**:* A tremendous actor.

(à lui) le pompon!	he's the tops!

*De toutes les petites voitures de sport, celle-ci tient **le pompon**!:* Of all the small sports cars this one beats them all!

il n'y a que ça	there's nothing to touch it

*Un bon whisky avant de se coucher, **il n'y a que ça**!:* There's nothing like a good whisky nightcap!

(après ça il faut) tirer l'échelle!	you can't beat that!

*Cinq médailles d'or. Après lui, on n'a qu'à **tirer l'échelle**!:* Five gold medals. Nobody is going to beat him; you might as well change your sport!

Excellence

mais quelle Byzance!   but what luxury!

Du saumon fumé, du caviar, du champagne! **Mais quelle Byzance,** *ma chère!:* Smoked salmon, caviar, champagne! But what luxury, my dear!

jeter un max   to make a great impression, to be the tops

Son blazer blanc à rayures rouges, ça **jette un max***:* His white blazer with red stripes is a knockout.

Excess/discontent

c'est le comble   that's the limit
c'est complet

il ne manquait plus que ça   that's the last straw

c'est la fin des haricots *   that really takes the biscuit

pour tout arranger   to cap it all (ironical)

Pour tout arranger *il commença à pleuvoir à verse!:* It began to pour with rain, which was all we needed!

en avoir marre *   to be fed up, browned off

*Toujours les mêmes questions! J'***en ai marre***!:* Always the same questions! I am fed up!

en avoir jusque là   to have had it up to here
en avoir ras le bol *   to be fed up to the back teeth
en avoir plein le dos
en avoir par-dessus la tête
en avoir plein les bottes
en avoir soupé

*J'***en ai par-dessus la tête** *de ces lettres:* I'm sick of these letters.

Expense

coûter les yeux de la tête

to cost the earth, an arm and a leg (It is interesting to compare the 'cost' in the two expressions: your eyes, or your arm and leg.)

le coup de fusil *

a rip-off, paying through the nose (restaurant), to pay over the top, to pay ridiculous prices

salé

stiff (bill)

la douloureuse

the bill (humorous, from 'douloureux' = painful)

f

face

la frimousse

(pretty little) face

la bobine

face, mug

*J'ai été innocenté mais tout le monde connaît ma **bobine** maintenant:* I was found innocent but everyone knows my face now.

la trogne

face (often the red one associated with drink)

*Un type à **la trogne** illuminée (d'avoir trop bu):* A chap with a glowing face (from too much drink).

avoir une tête à claques

to have the sort of silly face you feel like cuffing

failure

rater
louper *

to miss, fail

Failure

*Je ne veux pas **rater** mon examen:* I don't want to fail my exam.

tomber à l'eau   to fall through (plans)

ficher par terre *   to mess up

*Ça a tout **fichu par terre**!:* That's wrecked everything!

boire un bouillon   to suffer financially

le four   flop, failure (especially plays and films)

le bide *   flop, failure (especially show business)

*J'ai peur de faire un **bide**:* I'm afraid of a flop.

se ramasser *   to be a flop (especially show-business people)

se planter *   to fail, to get it wrong

*Il voulait être acteur mais il **s'est planté**:* He wanted to be an actor but he didn't make it.

remporter une veste   to suffer a setback

les carottes sont cuites *   it's all up
c'est cuit

*Et puis il a vu arriver un gendarme. «**C'est cuit**», m'a t-il soufflé:* And then he saw a policeman coming. 'We've had it', he whispered to me.

*Ses **carottes sont cuites**: He's had it now.*

se casser les dents sur   to come unstuck over something
quelque chose

*Eux aussi **se sont cassé les dents sur** ce problème délicat:* They too came to grief over this tricky problem.

finir en queue de poisson	to peter out
poser un lapin à quelqu'un	to miss a date, to stand someone up
être collé (à un examen)	to fail (an exam)
un fruit sec	a failure, dud (often of students)
le cafouillage	mess-up, shambles
la bérésina/Bérézina	disaster, mess, failure

*Le résultat de leur politique? Rien que des **Bérézina**!:* The result of their policy? One disaster after another.

To fall

ramasser une bûche/ une gamelle/un gadin une pelle prendre un billet de parterre	to take a tumble or figuratively to come a cropper

Il ramasse un gadin

To fall

valdinguer *   to go flying

*Vous pédalez trop vite. Attention, ou vous **valdinguez**!:* Don't pedal so fast. Watch out, or you'll take a header!

fear

le trac   fear, funk (normally 'trac' = stage fright)

*Au début j'ai dû vaincre mon **trac**:* At the beginning I had to overcome my fear.

avoir la frousse   to be really scared

la trouille *   funk

*Tu sais, les ascenseurs me fichent **la trouille**:* You know, lifts scare me stiff.

le trouillard *   coward

avoir les foies *   to be scared stiff

avoir la foire *   to be in a real panic
(la foire *)   (diarrhoea)

mouiller *   to be in a cold sweat, to be petrified

avoir les jetons   to be really jittery

*Il **a les jetons** devant cette aventure:* He is feeling scared about this adventure.

se dégonfler   to chicken out, lose one's nerve,
                                    climb down (much used
                                    expression)

*Surtout il ne faut pas avoir l'air de **se dégonfler** devant les copains:*
Above all you must not seem to chicken out in front of your pals.

je n'en menais pas large   I was quaking in my shoes, my
                                    knees were knocking

fickleness

retourner sa veste   to change one's view (suddenly),
                                    to change sides (as does a
                                    turncoat – 'veste' = jacket)

finality

un point, c'est tout   and that's that, that's final
un point, c'est marre *

*S'il est coupable il doit être puni, **un point c'est tout**!:* If he's guilty he
must be punished, and that's that!

point à la ligne   period, full stop, end of discussion
                                    (literally, full stop and new
                                    paragraph)

affaire classée   matter closed

*On a exigé des têtes – mais rien ne s'est passé.**Affaire classée**:* Heads
would have to roll – but nothing happened. That's the end of it.

flattery

faire de la lèche à   to flatter someone, to suck up to
quelqu'un   someone

Flattery

la brosse à reluire   flattery, soft-soap

*Mais je ne vais pas passer **la brosse à reluire** sur mes auteurs:* But I'm
not going to flatter my authors.

Food

l'amuse-gueule (m) **l'amuse-bouche**	cocktail snack, tasty titbit (less common but very polite)
les cochonailles (f)	cold meats
la patate	potato, spud
le fayot	bean
le bricheton *	bread
le frometon *	cheese

*«Quoi, pas de **frometon**?», cria Robert, toujours plutôt impoli:* 'Wot, no
cheese?', shouted Robert, as usual none too polite.

la bidoche *	meat
le canard	lump of sugar to be dipped in your brandy (A tradition that is still alive at least with the older generation living in the country.)
bouffer **croûter** * **grailler** * **croquer**	to eat, nosh (most common)
la bouffe **la boustifaille** **la soupe** **le frichti**	food, nosh

*Après on se fait une petite **bouffe**, hein?:* Afterwards what about a spot
of food together?

*L'heure de **la soupe**:* Time to eat, grub's up.

*Pour lui faire plaisir j'ai improvisé un **frichti** chez moi:* To please her I knocked up something to eat at home.

touiller   to stir

***Touiller** la soupe:* To stir round the soup.

manger sur le pouce   to have a quick bite, to grab
                                something to eat

casser la croûte   to have a snack, a bite
casser la graine *

*J'ai décidé de **casser la croûte** rapidement avant de partir:* I decided on a quick snack before leaving.

le petit déj   breakfast

*C'est par un **petit déj** énergétique que j'attaque la journée:* It is with a breakfast full of energy that I tackle the day ahead.

saucissonner   to have a (messy) picnic (typically
                                with cold meats and Beaujolais –
                                and of course a nice long loaf)

de l'étouffe-chrétien   heavy food, stodge, very ordinary
de la grosse cavalerie   food

faire la popote   to do the cooking

faire la tambouille   to cook, get some nosh ready

le rab *   extra, second helping (from
                                'rabiot', typical of army and
                                school vocabulary)

*Hé? Y a du **rab**?:* Hey, any seconds going?

se taper la cloche *   to have a slap-up meal

faire un gueuleton *   to have a really good tuck in

se goinfrer   to guzzle, stuff one's face

*Je l'ai vu **se goinfrer** d'éclairs:* I have seen him stuff his face with eclairs.

Food

manger au lance-pierre *   to bolt down one's food (with the image of it being catapulted into one's mouth)

avoir un bon coup de fourchette   to eat with relish, to enjoy one's food

caler sur le dessert   to be defeated by the pudding, dessert (because you've had enough and you can't get to the end)

le restau   restaurant

*Heureusement je peux me payer un bon **restau** de temps en temps:* Fortunately I can treat myself to a good restaurant from time to time.

le restau U   university canteen ('U' from 'Universitaire')

le self   self-service restaurant

la cantine   regular, local eating place (eaterie), restaurant (normally 'cantine' = canteen for business, schools etc.)

*Lorsque je suis en fonds, ma **cantine** préférée est le Ritz:* When I'm in funds I like going along to the Ritz for my meals.

Petites Révisions - Test Yourself!

PETITES REVISIONS 3
(Effort – Food)

Translations page 174

1. Ça va vous coûter les yeux de la tête.
2. Je suis un mordu de tennis et un jour je l'ai invitée à m'accompagner à Wimbledon. Bide!
3. Vas-y si tu veux mais ça ne me dit rien.
4. Chouette! On va skier. La neige est au poil.
5. C'est de la grosse cavalerie. Franchement, j'en ai marre.
6. Je vais rater mon train. Il ne manquerait plus que ça!
7. J'avais la frousse en descendant la pente surtout quand j'ai ramassé un gadin.
8. Tu te dégonfles? Alors c'est cuit.
9. On mange quelque chose sur le pouce avant de sortir.
10. Il y aura de la bonne bouffe, c'est sûr.

To play the fool

faire l'andouille to play the fool, act the giddy goat
faire le guignol
faire le zouave
faire le loustic

Forgiveness

passer l'éponge to wipe the slate clean

*Heureusement le directeur a bien voulu **passer l'éponge***: Fortunately the headmaster was willing to let bygones be bygones.

Free

à l'œil free, gratis, for nothing

*Tu veux dire que tu peux y manger **à l'œil**?*: You mean you can eat free there?

aux frais de la princesse free, on the house, on the firm

*Et quel boulot! Je voyage partout **aux frais de la princesse***: And what a job! I have free travel everywhere.

Frequency

trente-six (fois) countless, umpteen times

*J'ai essayé **trente-six** métiers*: I've tried heaps of jobs.

pour la énième fois for the umpteenth time

*Je leur écris **pour la énième fois**. J'attends toujours une réponse*: It's my umpteenth letter. I'm still waiting for an answer.

tous les trente-six du mois	once in a blue moon
une petite centaine de fois	heaps of times

Full up

bourré à craquer	bursting at the seams, crammed

Le théâtre était **bourré à craquer***: The theatre was packed out.*

plein comme un œuf	chock-a-block
truffé de	stuffed with

Son discours est **truffé de** *mots savants: His speech is stuffed with learned words.*

To make a fuss

faire une montagne **faire un monde** **faire un plat** **faire une tartine** * **faire un tabac** * **faire un fromage** * **faire des histoires** **faire une vie**	to make a fuss, a to-do

Faut pas te **faire un monde** *de tout ça: You mustn't blow the whole thing up.*

Il n'y a pas de quoi en **faire une tartine***: There is nothing to make a song and dance about.*

faire un foin terrible **faire du (un) tintamarre/** **du cinéma/du tam-tam**	to kick up a hell of a fuss (from the literal meaning of tom-tom)

La ville a **fait un** *grand* **tintamarre** *autour de la visite de la reine: The town made a great splash for the queen's visit.*

Les Anglais ont **fait du cinéma** *autour de cette affaire: There was a great to-do from the English about this matter.*

To make a fuss

il n'y a pas de quoi fouetter there's nothing to make a song
un chat and dance about

G

Grapevine

le téléphone arabe grapevine

*Tout le monde le sait grâce au **téléphone arabe** local:* Everyone
knows it thanks to the local grapevine.

Gratitude/favour

renvoyer l'ascenseur to pay back a favour

*«Compte sur moi», dit-il, mais il ne **renvoie** pas souvent **l'ascenseur**:*
'Count on me', he says, but he doesn't often return a favour.

donnant donnant help me and I'll do the same for
you

*Il pratique le **donnant donnant**:* If he does something for you, he
expects something in return.

faire une fleur (à quelqu'un) to do someone a favour

*Ils m'ont **fait une fleur**. Je peux continuer à manger avec mes
anciens collègues:* They did me a favour. I can continue to eat with my
former colleagues.

Greetings/questions/exclamations

salut! hi! cheers! hallo! (good) morning! (good) bye!

à la prochaine! till the next time (from 'à la prochaine fois')

au plaisir! be seeing you (from 'au plaisir de vous revoir')

ça biche? how are things? all well?
ça boume? *
ça gaze? *

à vos souhaits! bless you! (sneezing)

beurk! * yuk! ugh! oof!

A vos souhaits!

Greetings/questions/exclamations

Greetings/ questions/ exclamations

c'est dire!   that shows you!

Ce restaurant n'est pas dans les guides mais il paraît que le Premier Ministre y mange quelquefois. **C'est dire!**: This restaurant is not in the guides but apparently the Prime Minister sometimes goes there. That shows you!

chiche!   go on, I dare you! I bet you daren't

la ferme! *
ferme-la   shut up! give it a rest!

ça a été?   was it OK? (This is said of something nice and also, for example, to know if one has got through something unpleasant like an operation.)

«Ça a été?» *m'a demandé le garçon:* 'Did you enjoy that?' the waiter asked me.

laisse béton! *   lay off! drop it! don't carry on! (as in an argument – This is another example of verlan – see 'chébran' under *Character/attitude* – here for 'laisse tomber'.)

lâche-moi les baskets *   get off my back! leave me in peace!

en voiture Simone!   off we go! I must be away! I must hit the road! (A car is not a must.)

fouette cocher!   away we go (The figurative expression, with its image of the coachman or cabby whipping up his horses, has a certain dated flavour.)

J'achète d'abord un pied de lampe, ensuite une petite table – et **fouette cocher!** *Bientôt j'ai une belle collection d'antiquités:* I buy first a lampstand, next a little table – and off we go! Soon I have a fine collection of antiques.

82

qu'est-ce que tu fabriques?   what are you up to?

allez/va savoir   who knows?

*Et dans ces camions? Des armes, de l'or, **allez savoir**!:* And in these lorries? Weapons, gold, your guess is as good as mine!

***Va savoir** pourquoi!:* Who knows why!

Grumbling

râler   to grumble, moan

la grogne   moaning, grumbling

*Quelle est l'origine de **la grogne** actuelle?:* What is behind the present wave of discontent?

rouspéter   to grumble, protest, kick up a fuss (commonly used)

Gun

le pétard *   shooter

le flingue *   rifle, gun, pistol

H ────────────────────────

Hair

la tignasse   (head of) hair

les tifs (m) *   hair (on the head)

Haste/hurry

à la sauvette
with (indecent) haste, pretty quick (from the image of the illegal street trader who nips off on seeing the police – 'le vendeur à la sauvette'.)

*Les soldats ennemis sont partis **à la sauvette** avant l'aube:* The enemy soldiers made a quick getaway before dawn.

en catastrophe
in a wild rush, urgently, in a flap

*Il reprend l'avion **en catastrophe** pour Londres où l'attend le ministre:* He flies back to London in a rush where the minister is waiting for him.

il n'y a pas le feu
there's no great hurry

*Avoir des enfants? Bien sûr, mais **il n'y a pas le feu**:* Having children? Of course, but there's no rush.

faire vinaigre
to move pretty sharpish, to make haste

se remuer
to get a move on

***Remuez-vous** un peu!:* Make it snappy!

se grouiller
to get moving

***Grouille-toi** d'aller voir ce qui se passe:* Hurry up and see what's happening.

et que ça saute!
jump to it!

à la va-vite
hastily

*Je l'ai lu **à la va-vite**:* I skimmed through it.

To Help

dépanner quelqu'un   to help someone out (of a difficulty – such as 'une panne' = breakdown)

*Je n'avais plus de farine. Ma voisine m'a **dépannée**:* I had run out of flour. My neighbour came to the rescue.

mettre la main à la pâte   to lend a hand, to muck in

*Pour préparer ce festin, tout le monde a **mis la main à la pâte**:* To get this feast ready everybody joined in to help.

tomber pile   to come in handy

*Ce bistro ne ferme que tard et **tombera pile** si votre frigo est vide:* This little restaurant doesn't close until late and will be handy if your fridge is empty.

ça lui fera une belle jambe!   a lot of good that will do him!

sa mère lui a tout mâché   his mother did all the work for him, she gave it to him on a plate ('mâcher' = to chew)

Hesitation

se tâter   to dither

*Tu vas l'acheter? – Peut-être, je **me tâte**:* Are you going to buy it? _ Perhaps, I'm dithering.

sans faire ni une ni deux   without a moment's hesitation, without thinking twice about it

Hesitation

Chez moi dans mon pigeonnier

Home/room

l'appart (m)   flat (from 'appartement')

*Oui, j'ai le même petit **appart** avec vue sur la mer:* Yes, I have the same little flat with its sea view.

le pigeonnier	attic
un F3	a three-roomed flat
l'HLM (m/f)	'council' flat (from 'Habitation à Loyer Modéré')
les HLM	block (of council flats)
le clapier	small dump of a room, flat
la cage à lapins	'cage à lapins' can also refer to the whole block of such flats like so many rabbit hutches
le bocal *	pad, home
la crèche *	

la piaule *	room, place
la taule *	
la tanière	hideaway, bolt hole

*Une **tanière** de rêve:* An ideal hideaway.

percher *	to hang out
regagner ses pénates	to return home (literally, to one's household gods, as did the Romans)

Humility

courber l'échine	to bow and scrape, to grovel
faire des salamalecs	('l'échine' = backbone)
faire des courbettes	
faire des ronds de jambe	

Hunger

un petit creux	a touch of hunger

*Je sens venir **un petit creux**:* I'm beginning to feel pretty hungry.

creuser	to give an appetite

*Le footing, ça vous **creuse**:* Jogging gives you an appetite.

avoir l'estomac dans les talons	to feel ravenous
avoir une faim de loup	to be famished, to feel very hungry
crever de faim	to be starving
la fringale	stab of hunger

Hunger

**n'avoir rien à se mettre
sous la dent** not to have a bite to eat

Hurt

le bobo hurt, sore (from children's
language)

*Ça fait **bobo**?:* Does it hurt?

The French have some good road-safety slogans such as:

*Auto macho, auto **bobo**:* If you drive like a lad, you'll end up sad.

/ ▬▬▬▬▬▬▬▬▬▬▬▬▬▬▬▬▬▬▬▬▬

Illness/fitness

**se sentir un peu chose
ne pas être dans son
assiette
se sentir patraque** to feel a bit off form,
odd, under the weather

('assiette' originally meant one's
sitting position – so, if one is not
sitting comfortably …)

*C'est curieux. Quelquefois je dors bien mais **je me sens patraque** à
mon réveil:* It's curious. Sometimes I sleep well but I don't feel too good
when I wake up.

**ne pas se sentir très
vaillant** not to be feeling very fit

ne pas se sentir d'attaque not to be feeling up to the mark

tomber dans les pommes *
tourner de l'œil to pass out, flake out

*Quand j'ai vu le sang couler, j'ai failli **tomber dans les pommes**:*
When I saw the blood flowing I nearly passed out.

filer un mauvais coton	to be in a sorry state,
être mal en point	in a poor way
il va tout doux	he's fair, middling
être dans les vapes *	to be out for the count from drinks or drugs (from 'les vapeurs' = vapours)
avoir un sérieux mal de crâne	to have a nasty 'head'
être sur le flanc	to be laid up
attraper la crève	to catch one's death
ça sent le sapin *	he/she's not long to go, he/she won't last long now ('Sapin' evokes the wood of the coffin.)
se crever *	to wreck oneself, ruin one's health
l'œil poché (m)	black eye
l'œil au beurre noir	
le cocard	
l'hosto (m) *	hospital
le billard *	operating table (the 'billiard-table' image)

Impatience

poireauter *	to hang around waiting
faire le pied de grue	('la grue' = crane bird)
moisir *	

*A quoi bon **moisir** ici?*: What's the point of hanging around here?

minute papillon! *	half a mo! hold on a moment! hold it!

Impatience

vivement   hurry on, roll on

Vivement *un double whisky!:* I can't wait for a large whisky.

Vivement *le 14 juillet:* Hurry on the 14th of July.

Vivement *que tout rentre dans l'ordre:* May everything soon get back to normal.

Petites Révisions – Test Yourself!

PETITES REVISIONS 4
(To play the Fool – Impatience)

Translations page 174

1. On peut y entrer à l'œil. Il me l'a dit pour la énième fois.
2. Il n'y a pas de quoi fouetter un chat. Mais lui, il veut toujours rouspéter.
3. J'ai essayé trente-six fois d'arrêter de fumer.
4. «Ça biche?» m'a-t-il dit comme toujours.
5. Bien sûr il faut visiter les musées. Mais il n'y a pas le feu!
6. J'ai fait le pied de grue pendant quelque temps mais personne n'est arrivé.
7. Après l'accident je suis allé le voir dans sa piaule. Heureusement pas de bobo.
8. Je sens venir un petit creux alors je regagne mes pénates.
9. Quel vent froid! De quoi attraper la crève!
10. Je n'y vais pas. Je ne me sens pas dans mon assiette ce matin.

Impertinence

gonflé   with a nerve

*Il est **gonflé** ce type-là!:* What a nerve that chap has got!

le toupet   cheek
le culot

*Il a tous les **toupets**:* He's a hell of a cheek.

culotté   cheeky

il ne manque pas d'air!   he's a cheeky blighter!

faire un pied de nez   to cock a snook

*En écrivant cela il a **fait un pied de nez** aux pouvoirs publics:* In
writing that he cocked a snook at the authorities.

Il fait un pied de nez

Importance

faire la une   to be front-page news

*Le lendemain ça a **fait la une** des journaux:* The next day it was splashed across the front pages.

le ténor   big noise, star performer

un gros bonnet   big noise, VIP
une grosse légume *   (normally 'un légume')
une huile

*Aujourd'hui c'est une figure médiatique, **une grosse légume**:* Today he is a media figure, a big noise.

le grand manitou   the big boss who calls the shots

le ponte   big shot

*Un **ponte** du show-business:* A big noise in show-business.

le beau linge   top people, 'beautiful people'

*Demain soir à l'opéra il y aura du **beau linge**:* There will be top people at the opera tomorrow night.

le gratin   top society, the best
le dessus du panier
la crème

le super gratin   the very cream of society, the really top people

le sous-fifre   underling, chief cook and bottle washer

*Il refuse de me recevoir. Je dois aller en parler à un **sous-fifre**:* He refuses to see me. I have to go and discuss it with an underling.

compter pour du beurre   to count for nothing, to be of no account

*Il me l'avait promis mais cela **comptait pour du beurre**:* He had promised it to me but that didn't mean anything.

il ne se mouche pas du coude	he does himself well, he lays on the style
il croit que c'est arrivé **il se croit sorti de la cuisse de Jupiter** **il se prend pour le nombril du monde**	he thinks he's the cat's whiskers
faire la mouche du coche	to be as busy as a bee, in a tiresome and ineffective way (The expression comes from a fable by La Fontaine.)
se poser là	to be really capable, impressive

*Comme raconteur, il **se pose** un peu **là**!:* He's really quite a story teller!

ça vous pose!	that makes you into someone!

*Un jet privé, **ça vous pose!**:* With a private jet you really are someone!

c'est pour la frime	it's just for show, it's just to impress

*Il a horreur de l'eau. Sa piscine, **c'est pour la frime**!:* He hates water. His swimming pool is just for show!

Indifference

s'en ficher **s'en foutre** * **s'en taper** * **s'en tamponner** * **s'en moquer comme de l'an quarante**	not to care about (something) (impolite usage)

*Je m'en **fiche** pas mal:* I couldn't care less.

je m'assois dessus! *	I am damned if I care about it!
bof!	pooh! see if I care!

Indifference

Quelques-uns parlent de la **bof** génération: Some talk of the 'so what?' generation.

connais pas! I'm not interested, it never occurs to me, I don't give it a thought

Boire tout seul, **connais pas**: I never think of drinking on my own.

faire comme si ... to act as if nothing had happened, to carry on as before

Cela nous a bouleversés. Mais que faire? On en a parlé et on a décidé de **faire comme si** *(ça n'était pas arrivé):* That upset us. But what was to be done? We spoke about it and decided to carry on regardless.

Influence

le piston pull, influence

Je ne veux pas utiliser **le piston** *de mon père:* I don't want to use my father's influence.

se faire pistonner to get strings pulled

Innocence

gober to 'swallow', believe everything you hear

Elle **gobe** *tout!:* She believes everything you tell her!

avoir l'air de ne pas y toucher to look as innocent as anything

avoir un air de sainte nitouche ('nitouche' = 'n'y touche')

| **on lui donnerait le bon Dieu sans confession** | butter wouldn't melt in his/her mouth (Such an innocent look means obviously that there is no sin to confess.) |

| **ne pas être tombé de la dernière pluie** **ne pas être né d'hier** | to be no innocent, to have been around |

| **un enfant de chœur** **une enfant de Marie** | a naïve and innocent person |

*J'ai compris très vite que leur fils, bien que fort poli, n'était pas **un enfant de chœur**:* I quickly understood that their son, though very polite, was no angel.

| **croire au Père Noël** | to be blissfully innocent, naïve |

| **mine de rien** | innocently, quite casually |

*Il lève la main, très **mine de rien**, pour poser la question-piège:* He raises his hand, looking ever so innocent, to ask the trick question.

Insults/swearing

| **le mot de cinq lettres (M.E.R.D.E.)** | four-letter word |

*C'est vrai que cette jeune recrue a dit les **cinq lettres** au colonel?:* Is it true that this young recruit used a four-letter word to the colonel?

| **merde!** | standard four-letter word (The literal meaning is 'excrement'. It is much used in various contexts, for while usually distinctly impolite, it can be at times mild, even humorous. It can even be used to wish someone luck. If that seems odd, are not bird droppings sometimes considered lucky, and do we not wish people 'mud in the eye'?) |

Insults/swearing

le mot de Cambronne

This is a euphemism for the above, after General Cambronne who, on being asked to surrender at Waterloo, gave this curt answer – so it is related.

va te faire cuire un œuf! *
va te faire voir! *
va te rhabiller! *

go and get stuffed!
get lost!

*Il tourna les talons en me disant d'**aller me rhabiller**:* He turned on his heels telling me to get lost.

le bras d'honneur

two fingers sign

salaud!

swine!

espèce de ...

(gives added force to insults)

Espèce d'idiot!:* You stupid fool!

traiter quelqu'un de tous les noms

to call someone every name under the sun

Interest/expertise

ça me/nous connaît

I/we know all about it

L'électroménager? **ça nous connaît**:* We are the experts on electrical appliances.

c'est dans mes cordes
c'est mon rayon

it's up my street, just my line,
it's just right for me

*Il aurait dû me téléphoner. Le bricolage **c'est dans mes cordes**:* He should have phoned me. Odd-job handywork is just up my street.

Interference

marcher sur les plates-bandes de quelqu'un	to trespass on someone else's patch ('plate-bande' = flower bed)

Intolerance

je ne peux pas le sentir	I can't stick the sight of him
je ne peux pas le gober	I can't bear him
je ne peux pas le blairer *	
je ne peux pas le voir en peinture	

J

Joke

la blague	joke, leg-pull

*Sans **blague**?*: You don't mean it?

***Blague** dans le coin*: Seriously, no joking?

*Une **blague** de potache*: A schoolboy's prank.

le poisson d'avril	April fool (In France the fish is the traditional symbol for 1st April, so apart from the usual leg-pulls, you may actually find that a mock fish has been attached to your back!)

*Les élèves étaient bien sages et attentifs. J'étais encore plus sûr qu'ils allaient me faire un **poisson d'avril***: The pupils were very well behaved and attentive. I was even more sure that they were going to April-fool me.

Joke

On lui fait un poisson d'avril

le canulard   hoax, leg-pull

*La police croit plutôt à un **canulard***:The police think it's more likely a hoax.

faire des siennes   to be at it again

*Zut! Le démarreur re**fait des siennes**!:* Blow! The starter is playing up again!

Kindness

sympa   nice, kind, decent (from
chic   'sympathique')

*Un prof peu **sympa***: Not a very nice teacher.

*Chez nous des prix **sympas***: You'll like our prices.

| **le papa gâteau** | father who indulges his child |
| **la B.A.** | good deed (from 'Bonne Action') |

*Elle aime mieux que je ne parle pas de ses **B.A.**:* She'd rather I didn't mention her good deeds.

Kiss

| **la bise** | kiss on the cheek (usually means 'cold north wind') |
| **le bisou** * | kiss, peck |

*Après les **bisous** d'adieu:* After the farewell embraces.

Kit / gear

| **le barda** **le fourbi** | kit, gear, clobber |
| **le bataclan** **le Saint-Frusquin** | also used in the sense of 'all the rest' |

*Il est parti sous la pluie avec son **barda** sur les épaules:* He went off in the rain with his gear on his shoulders.

*Et tout **le bataclan**!:* The whole damned lot!

Knowledge / information

| **le tuyau** | tip |

*Un **tuyau** increvable:* A hot tip.

| **les infos (f)** | news, information, info (from 'informations') |

*Chaque matin j'écoute **les infos** routières:* Each morning I listen to the traffic news.

Knowledge/information

être dans le coup   to be in on it

être au parfum *   to be in the know, to know what's going on, what's afoot

*Seuls quelques ministres **sont au parfum***: Only a few ministers are in the know.

connaître les ficelles   to know the ropes

en connaître un bout   to know a thing or two
en connaître un rayon

*Quant à la bonne cuisine, les Français **en connaissent un bout***: When it comes to good cooking the French certainly know something.

être une vraie gazette   to know all the local news

*Je sais tout ce qui se passe dans le quartier grâce à Henri – **une vraie gazette***: I know everything that goes on locally thanks to Henri – he knows it all.

être calé (en)   to be well up (in), to be knowledgeable, hot stuff

montrer patte blanche   to show one's credentials (pass, identity etc.)

le B.A. – BA   basics, first steps (reference to learning how to read)

*Le **B.A. – BA** du secourisme*: First steps in first aid.

l'intox (f)   misinformation, brainwashing (from 'intoxication')

L'intox dans nos écoles? Mais non! C'est pas vrai: Brainwashing in our schools? Not at all! It's not true.

être payé pour le savoir   to know it to one's cost

connaître la musique   to know the score

être fixé   to be in the picture

*Envoyez une lettre et vous **serez fixé** tout de suite:* Send a letter and you'll be put wise at once.

les biscuits (m) *   information

*Si mon avocat est optimiste, c'est sans doute grâce aux **biscuits** que lui seul possède:* If my barrister is optimistic, it is doubtless because of the info that he alone has.

je vous le donne en mille   guess away, you'll never get it

inconnu au bataillon   never 'eard of him (her, them, it)

*Un jour je demande des croissants. **Inconnus au bataillon**:* One day I ask for croissants. They never have such things.

Land

le plancher des vaches   terra firma, dry land

Il préfère rester sur le plancher des vaches

Laziness

avoir la flemme	to feel lazy
tirer sa flemme	to laze around
avoir un poil dans la main	to have a lazy streak
tirer au flanc	to skive
le tire-au-flanc	skiver
glander * **glandouiller ***	to loaf around

*Le dimanche je **glande**:* On Sundays I just loaf around.

coincer la bulle *	to do nothing
peigner la girafe *	to do nothing much, to fritter away one's time
se les rouler *	not to do a damned thing, to have it easy
feignant	lazybones ('feignant' can be a noun or adjective and is the familiar form of 'fainéant' i.e. faire + néant (nothing))
se tourner les pouces	to twiddle one's thumbs

*Il devrait recommencer au lieu de **se tourner les pouces** en attendant que son père l'aide:* He should start again instead of twiddling his thumbs while waiting for his father to help him.

ne rien faire de ses dix doigts	not to do a hand's turn

Limitation

être réduit à la portion congrue	to be down to the minimum, the bare essentials

*L'avion est bourré d'électronique ce qui **réduit** le cockpit **à la portion congrue**:* The plane is stuffed with electronics which means there's only just room in the cockpit.

pour tout potage   all told

*Ce soir là dans le frigo, j'avais **pour tout potage** un peu de pâté:* That evening, all I had in the fridge was a bit of pâté.

Luck

le veinard   lucky devil

*Alors tu ne travailles que cinq jours par semaine. **Veinard**!:* So you only work five days a week. Lucky thing!

la veine   (good) luck
le pot
la baraka   (Arabic word)
la pêche
le bol *

*Un coup de **pot**:* A stroke of luck.

*On me libère tout de suite. C'est la première de mes **barakas**:* I'm freed at once. That't the first of my lucky breaks.

*Ils ont une **pêche** de débutants:* They have beginners' luck.

être verni   to be really lucky, to have luck on one's side

être né coiffé   to be born lucky

tirer le bon numéro   to come up lucky

je leur souhaite bien   and the best of luck to
du plaisir!   them! and I wish them luck! (ironical)

la déveine   bad luck
la poisse *
la guigne

Luck

la scoumoune

*Ma **guigne** c'est de ne pas avoir fait leur connaissance plus tôt:* It was my bad luck not to have met them earlier.

*Je me demande s'il n'a pas **la scoumoune**:* I wonder if he isn't dogged by bad luck.

la tuile	bad luck, blow, nasty shock (as if a tile had fallen on your head!)
ne pas être gâté	to be out of luck

*Deux jours de pluie. On n'est vraiment **pas gâté**:* Two days of rain. We are not having much luck.

un jour sans	a luckless day

*Nous avons bien joué, mais c'était **un jour sans**:* We played well but it was just one of those days.

toucher du bois	to touch wood
croiser les doigts	to cross one's fingers

*Il **croise** et recroise **les doigts** avant d'y entrer:* He keeps crossing his fingers before going in.

M

Mad/stupid

cinglé **dingue**	crazy, nuts (commonly used)
maboul **raide fou**	mad, off one's rocker

les tordus (m)	loonies
le fada	nut case
fou à lier	mad as a hatter
le ballot	clot, muggins
la gourde	
la bille	
le nœud *	git, idiot

*On nous prend pour des **billes**:* They take us for fools.

*T'es le vrai **nœud**:* You really are a git.

foufou	a bit scatty, a bit bonkers
farfelu	a bit odd, weird, a bit crazy
loufoque	
timbré	cracked
fêlé	
avoir un petit vélo dans la tête *	to have a few screws loose
con *	damned stupid (very commonly used)

*Etre **con** comme la lune:* To be a complete idiot.

demeuré	not all there

*Mais qu'est-ce qu'il a? Faut être vraiment **demeuré** pour faire ça:* But what's wrong with him? You've got to be really dim to do that.

déménager	to be round the bend (literally to move house)
perdre la boule	to go off one's nut
à question idiote, réponse idiote	ask a silly question and you'll get a silly answer

To Marry

convoler   to get hitched (humorous)

Il voulait savoir si j'étais toujours architecte, où j'habitais, si j'avais
***convolé**...*: He wanted to know if I was still an architect, where I lived, if I
had taken a wife...

passer devant Monsieur   to get married (It's the mayor who
le Maire   performs the legal ceremony.)

Me/ myself

ma pomme *   me, myself
bibi *

*C'est pour qui? Pour **bibi**:* Who's it for? For me.

votre serviteur   yours truly

*Le voleur se sauve suivi par **votre serviteur**:* The thief makes off
followed by yours truly.

Misfortune/ suffering

écoper   to cop it

*Elle a **écopé** d'une amende de deux cents francs:* She got landed with a
two-hundred-franc fine.

trinquer   to cop it, suffer, pay the price

*C'est les profs qui **trinquent**:* It's the teachers who are going through it.

y laisser des plumes   to suffer a loss (often financial),
                                       not to escape unscathed

*On ne voulait pas l'écouter mais il avait dit plus d'une fois que l'Angleterre **y laisserait des plumes***: Nobody would listen to him but he said more than once that England would not emerge unscathed.

Mistakes

l'impair (m)
la bourde
la gaffe
blunder, bloomer

*Il a fait une **gaffe***: He dropped a brick.

la bavure
le couac
slip-up, blunder (often political)

*On crie déjà à **la bavure***: They are already saying someone has slipped up.

*Que va dire le ministre? On attend **le couac***: What will the minister say? They are waiting for him to put his foot in it.

se mettre le doigt dans l'œil
to get it all wrong, to be on the wrong track

mettre les pieds dans le plat to put one's foot in it

se gourer
to be mistaken

*On est sûr de ne pas **se gourer** si on dit que ça coûtera plus cher l'année prochaine*: You certainly won't boob if you say it will be dearer next year.

mettre à côté de la plaque   to be off track, to get it wrong

*Si vous pensez que je n'aime plus le cinéma, vous **mettez à côté de la plaque**. Rien ne vaut un bon film à mon avis*: If you think I no longer care for the cinema, you are wide of the mark. There is nothing like a good film, in my opinion.

Money

le fric	cash, dough (especially common)
la galette *	
le pognon *	
l'oseille (f) *	(normally 'l'oseille' = sorrel)
le pèze *	
le blé *	
les écus (m)	
les gros sous	
le nerf de la guerre	('la guerre' = war: wars cost money)

*Ils sont bourrés de **fric***: They're loaded.

*Une question d'**écus***: A question of money.

*Un problème de **gros sous***: A matter of cash.

*A cette époque il était démuni du **nerf de la guerre***: At that time he was short of money.

casquer	to cough up, to fork out
cracher	

*Son père continue à **casquer***: His father goes on forking out.

se fendre de quelque chose	to fork out for something
le fils à papa	son of a powerful and wealthy father
huppé	well off

*Une clientèle **huppée***: Well-heeled guests.

les gros (m)	the rich
le richard	wealthy chap
faire son beurre	to make one's pile
faire sa pelote	
le magot	cash stashed away, hoard

*Bien sûr ils refusent de dire où ils ont caché **le magot***: Of course they refuse to say where the loot has been stashed away.

être en fonds	to be in funds
une coquette somme de deux mille francs	a tidy sum of two thousand francs
mettre du beurre dans ses épinards	to help things along, to make life a bit more pleasant

*Je garde les pourboires, alors ça **met du beurre dans les épinards***: I keep the tips; it all helps (as does butter in the spinach).

ce n'est pas le Pérou	it's no gold mine, it's no big deal. {Peru was seen as the country of riches.)

*On me paie un peu. **Ce n'est pas le Pérou** mais ça va*: I am paid a little. I shan't get rich on it but I manage.

gagner sa croûte **gagner son steak** **assurer sa matérielle**	to earn one's living, bread and butter (Bread and butter sounds better than crust but not as good as steak! Le 'steak-frites' (chips) is comparable to our 'meat and two veg'.)
l'ardoise (f)	account (from the time when tick was marked on slates)

***L'ardoise** va être salée*: You'll have a lot to pay off.

le panier percé	spendthrift
taper quelqu'un	to touch someone for money
en mettre à gauche	to save up, put money on one side

*Un conseil. **Mets-en à gauche***: One bit of advice. Put some money on one side.

au prix où est le beurre	prices being what they are (butter being an important item on the shopping list)

Money

boucler ses fins/sa fin de mois to make ends meet at the end of the month

*Ah! Un petit chèque! Ça aidera à **boucler ma fin de mois**!:* Ah! A little cheque! That will help to keep my head above water.

un sou est un sou a penny is a penny and they all add up

claquer son argent/fric to blow one's money

*Elle **claque son fric** en fringues:* She blows all her money on clothes.

croquer ses éconocroques (f) * to blue all one's savings

le bas de laine nest egg (The woollen stocking evokes the image of money carefully kept at home. Compare our 'under-the-mattress' philosophy.)

mettre au clou to pawn

n'avoir plus un rond not to have a bean left
n'avoir plus un radis (normally 'radis' = radish)

être dans la dèche to be hard up
être dans la purée

ne pas avoir un rouge liard not to have a brass farthing

être fauché (comme les blés) to be broke (much used)

*Ils étaient **fauchés** en permanence:* They were always broke.

être à fond de cale to be on one's beam ends

être sans un to be penniless

tirer le diable par la queue to be hard up

*Je les plains. Ils **tirent le diable par la queue** depuis longtemps:* I feel sorry for them. They've been hard up for ages.

n

The call of Nature

faire pipi	to spend a penny, to pee
le petit coin	loo
les waters (m)	(from 'water closet')
les vessés (m)	(from 'W.C.' curiously pronounced)
les chiottes (f) *	bog
aller où le roi va seul	to go … you know where

A Near thing

on a eu chaud　　　　　it was a close call

*La sentinelle nous a vus et a tiré deux fois. **On a eu chaud**:* The sentry saw us and fired twice. It was a close call.

il était moins cinq/une　　it was a near thing, a close shave

*Soudain j'ai vu l'enfant. J'ai appuyé à fond sur la pédale de frein. **Il était moins une**!:* Suddenly I saw the child. I stamped on the brake pedal. It was a narrow squeak.

revenir de loin　　　　　to have been touch and go, to have been on the brink (often of illness)

Negation

pas pour un/deux sou(s)   not in the least

*Il n'est pas sportif **pour un sou**:* He isn't the least little bit athletic.

Never

la semaine des quatre   never
jeudis
à Pâques ou à la Trinité

*Il a fait faillite. Tu recevras son chèque **la semaine des quatre jeudis**:* He has gone bankrupt. You'll never see his cheque.

quand les poules auront   when pigs can fly
des dents

attendre jusqu'à la   to wait until the cows come home
Saint-Glinglin *

renvoyer/remettre aux   to put off indefinitely
calendes (grecques)

*Chaque jour je le **remets aux calendes**:* Every day I keep putting it off to some other time.

Nonsense

des balançoires (f)   nonsense, rubbish, wild talk,
des salades (f) *   eyewash
des foutaises (f) *
le bla-bla   waffle

***Foutaises** que tout cela!:* Baloney!

*Un guide qui est pratique et sans **bla-bla**:* A practical guidebook which is free of waffle.

déconner *   to talk drivel

To Note

inscrire/mettre quelque   to make a note of something, to
chose sur ses tablettes   jot down

*Bon, lundi à dix heures. Je vais **inscrire** ça **sur mes tablettes**:* Right, Monday at ten. I'll make a note of it.

Il l'a inscrit sur ses tablettes

Nothing/ hardly anything

des clopinettes *   not a damned thing
que dalle *

T'as compris? **Que dalle**!: Did you understand? Not a damned thing!

pour des prunes   for nothing
pour le roi de Prusse

*Travailler **pour le roi de Prusse**:* To work for nothing, no return, for nowt.

trois fois rien   next to nothing

*Les détectives ont cherché presque en vain – un fil, un mégot, **trois fois rien**:* The detectives searched almost in vain – a piece of thread, a cigarette end, hardly anything at all.

Obedience

faire du zèle   to be super keen

être pète-sec   to be sharp, authoritative, strict

exécution!   go and do it! see to it! get on with it! go to it!

| **être service-service** | to stick to the rules, to be very officious |
| **être jugulaire** | |

Le directeur est service-service

Opportunity

| **sauter sur l'occase** | to jump at the chance (from 'occasion') |

| **prendre le train en marche** | to jump onto the bandwagon |

*Ils ont **pris en marche le train** de ces méthodes «sans grammaire» à la plus grande joie de bon nombre d'enfants:* They have jumped onto the bandwagon of these 'no-grammar' methods to the delight of many children.

| **vouloir le beurre et l'argent du beurre** | to want to have one's cake and eat it |

| **rater le coche** | to miss the boat (In the old days it was indeed the coach which had to be caught.) |

Petites Révisions - Test Yourself!

PETITES REVISIONS 5
(Impertinence - Opportunity)

Translations page 175

1. On attend le départ des grosses légumes.
2. A ma surprise il lui a dit le mot de Cambronne.
3. Ça m'intéresse. C'est dans mes cordes.
4. Impossible d'y entrer sans montrer patte blanche.
5. J'ai eu du pot. Mon cousin connaît les ficelles et il m'a donné quelques tuyaux.
6. Ce billet de cent balles est pour bibi!
7. Ça m'aide à gagner mon steak.
8. Il m'a dit qu'il était fauché.
9. Il faut sauter sur l'occase si tu as assez de fric.
10. Cette fois il s'est mis le doigt dans l'œil.

P

Paris

Paname *   Paris

*Je ne te verrai pas puisque je ne passe pas par **Paname**:* I shan't see you since I'm not going through Paris.

parigot *   Parisian (pejorative)

*Un accent **parigot**:* A Parisian accent.

People

le type **le gars**	chap
le mec * **le gonze** * **le citoyen** * **le pèlerin** *	bloke

*Mais dis donc! Ces **mecs** vont rester là sur la route à bavarder?:* But I say! Are those blokes going to stand there on the road chatting?

la gonzesse * **la pépée** * **la nana** * **la souris** *	female, bird
le cuistot	cook
le gabelou	customs officer
le resquilleur	cheat (who gets in free, queue-barges)

*C'est un **resquilleur** qui a «oublié» son carton d'invitation:* He's a gate-crasher who has 'forgotten' his invitation card.

People

le/la réac reactionary (from 'réactionnaire')

*Les élèves ne l'aiment pas beaucoup. Un **réac**, disent-ils:* The pupils don't much care for him. One of the old school, they say.

le pipelet concierge, caretaker

le rond-de-cuir clerk (The image is of a punctilious one sitting on his round leather cushion.)

l'écolo (m/f) environmentalist (from 'écologiste')

les ados (m/f) teenagers (from 'adolescents')

*Un petit groupe d'**ados** chacun avec son baladeur sur les oreilles:* A little group of teenagers each with his walkman on his head.

le vieux routier old hand (who knows it all)

le monstre sacré pin-up, idol, star

*Un **monstre sacré** du football anglo-saxon:* A star of English football.

Les ados

Le clodo

le clodo *   tramp

*D'autres femmes auraient eu peur en rencontrant ce **clodo** un peu ivre:* Other women would have been afraid on meeting this tramp who had had rather too much to drink.

le carabin   medical student, medic

le gai luron   jolly fellow
le joyeux drille

*Deux **gais lurons** s'il en fut:* Two likely lads if ever there were.

le loustic   odd bod, joker, wag

le croquant   peasant
le plouc *

le pignouf *   boorish lout

le cabotin   poor actor

le kinési   physio (from 'kinésithérapeute')

l'ophtalmo (m/f)   eye specialist (from 'ophtalmologiste')

*Le test **ophtalmo**:* Eye test.

People

la perle   treasure

*Louise fait tout pour moi. C'est une **perle**:* Louise does everything for me. She's a treasure.

l'intello (m/f)   intellectual (from 'intellectuel')

*C'est Jules **l'intello** de ce trio:* Jules is the brainy guy of the three.

le gorille   body guard, minder (see under
le porte-flingue *   *Gun*)

*«En ce cas-là je vais vous faire dégager», et il fit signe à ses deux **gorilles**:* 'In that case I'll get you removed', and he beckoned to his two minders.

l'aubergine (f)   (female) traffic warden, meter
                                     maid
la pervenche   (from the colour of the uniform,
                                     'pervenche' = periwinkle)

le paumé   drop-out

le minet   elegantly dressed young man
                                     (over concerned with his
                                     appearance)

la minette   dolled-up young girl

le routard   (young) backpacker

*Les beaux jours arrivent et les **routards** se mettent en route:* The fine weather arrives and the young backpackers set off on their travels.

le plongeur   washer-up (in a restaurant)

la barbouze *   secret agent

le/la mytho   dreamer, tall story teller (from
                                     'mythomane')

*Il nous a dit qu'il était millionnaire et un ami du Président. C'est un **mytho**!:* He told us he was a millionaire and a friend of the President. It's one of his make-believe stories.

la petite fille à sa maman   sissy

*Mais si un garçon refuse de le faire, c'est vraiment **la petite fille à sa maman**:* But if a boy refuses, he's a real sissy.

Police

le flic	cop (The American TV programme 'Miami Vice' was called «Deux Flics à Miami».)
le motard	motorcycle cop
l'indic (m)	informer, grass (from 'indicateur')
le mouchard	snitch
la souricière	police trap

*Une **souricière** a été tendue dans l'immeuble:* The police set a trap in the building.

le panier à salade	Black Maria (police van)
épingler	to nab
pincer	
coincer	

*La police le connaît mais il n'a jamais été **coincé**:* The police know him but he has never been nicked.

se faire embarquer	to get picked up, arrested
se faire cueillir	
se faire coffrer	to get locked up
la brigade des stups	drug squad (from 'stupéfiants')
la planque	stake-out

*Ils ont organisé une **planque** devant l'hôtel:* They staked out the hotel.

Police

le lacrymo   tear gas (from 'gaz lacrymogène')

*Pas de **lacrymo**, raconte un manifestant, mais ils ont tiré des balles en caoutchouc. Il n'y a pas eu de blessés:* No tear gas, a demonstrator relates, but they used rubber bullets. Nobody was hurt.

filer quelqu'un   to shadow someone

semer quelqu'un   to throw off, lose, shed someone
                                   following

*Ce n'est qu'en arrivant dans la vieille ville que j'ai pu les **semer**:* It was only when I got to the old town that I was able to shake them off.

Popularity

le chouchou   favourite, pet
la coqueluche   ('la coqueluche' = whooping
                                   cough in standard French)

*Il est **la coqueluche** de toutes les vieilles dames du quartier:* All the old ladies around here adore him.

s'arracher   to be in great demand

*On se l'**arrache** :* It/he/she is much in demand.

*Soudain on **s'arrache** les voitures de luxe:* Suddenly people are falling over themselves to get luxury cars.

Position

(la) lanterne rouge   the rear, tail-end

*En ce moment les joueurs du Nord sont **lanterne rouge**:* At the moment the players from the North are trailing.

Pretence

bidon   bogus, phoney

*Un numéro de rue **bidon**:* A bogus street number.

c'est du toc   it's sham

*Ce diamant? **C'est du toc**!:* This diamond? It's a fake!

en toc   sham

*Des millionnaires **en toc**:* 'Pretend' millionaires.

c'est du chiqué   it's a sham, a try-on

*Le type nous menace, mais mon mari me chuchote: «**C'est du chiqué.**»:* The chap threatens us but my husband whispers: 'He's bluffing.'

(faire) du cinéma   to put on an act, a show, a
                                    performance, to stage a scene

*Mon Dieu! Ils se querellent et ce n'est pas **du cinéma**!:* Good Heavens! They are quarrelling and it's for real!

Prison

à l'ombre   in jail, jug

*Je sais qu'ils ont passé quelque temps **à l'ombre**:* I know they spent some time inside.

le violon*   police cells

le trou *   jail, jug
la taule *
la cabane *

*Ils ont fait trois mois de **cabane**:* They did three months in jail.

Prison

le taulard *	jailbird
le cheval de retour	old lag (who keeps coming back)
la planque *	hide-out
le mouton *	'plant' (in a cell)
se faire la belle *	to escape (from prison)

*Un prisonnier **se fait la belle** à bicyclette. Incroyable!:* A prisoner breaks out on a bicycle. Incredible!

être en cavale *	to be on the run, to have done a runner

To Put down/silence someone

rabattre le caquet à quelqu'un	to put someone down
clouer le bec à quelqu'un	to shut someone up

Q

Quantity and intensification

pas mal	lots, quite a lot

*Il a **pas mal** d'amis ici:* He has quite a lot of friends here.

le tas	heap, pile

*Il y en a des **tas**:* There are heaps.

la flopée *	mass

*Il y en a des **flopées**:* There are oodles.

des régiments
masses

*Je n'ai plus peur **des régiments** d'insectes qui courent partout dans ma chambre:* I am no longer afraid of the hordes of insects running all over my room.

il n'y en a pas des masses
there are not many, they are thin on the ground

*Je cherche un débit de tabac depuis dix minutes. **Il n'y en a pas des masses** par ici:* I have been looking for a tobacconist for ten minutes. They are hard to find round here.

ne pas se trouver sous le pas d'une mule
to be hard to come by, to be pretty rare

*Un jeune homme sérieux, charmant et talentueux. Un fiancé comme ça, on n'en trouve pas **sous le pas d'une mule**, tu sais!:* A serious, charming and talented young man. You don't find a fiancé like that everywhere, you know!

la brochette
knot, bunch

*Une **brochette** de banquiers:* A group of bankers.

(en avoir) à revendre
to have to spare

*Il a du charme **à revendre**:* He has masses of charm.

j'en passe et des meilleures
and many more I could mention

*Il avoue plusieurs crimes – vol, recel, chantage. **J'en passe et des meilleures**:* He admits to several crimes – theft, receiving, blackmail. I'll gloss over the rest.

la kyrielle
throng, string, crowd (of people)

*Une **kyrielle** de plaintes:* A string of complaints.

(toute) la lyre
the (whole) lot

Quantity and intensification

On a parlé de ses défauts. **Toute la lyre!**: We spoke of his faults. We went through the lot.

trois pelés et un tondu just the odd few (people), just a few characters (of no distinction)

les gros bataillons bulk, masses

Les gros bataillons *de cette somme iront au gouvernement:* The bulk of this sum will go to the government.

une paille! peanuts!

Un million de francs! **Une paille!**: A million francs! A mere nothing!

à gogo masses, galore
à la pelle

Le soleil **à gogo**: Lots and lots of sun.

Quel match! Des buts **à la pelle**!: What a match! Goals galore!

comme s'il en pleuvait plenty, masses, heaps

Il y avait de belles voitures **comme s'il en pleuvait**: There were beautiful cars everywhere.

moult many a (from Latin 'multum' dated but used with a touch of humour)

Après **moult** *consultations:* After many a consultation.

un doigt/un dé/une larme a drop of wine
de vin

un soupçon de lait a touch of milk
un nuage (de lait)

Très peu de lait pour moi, s'il vous plaît. **Un nuage.** *C'est ça. Merci:* Very little milk for me please. Just a spot. That's right. Thank you.

Un nuage de lait

une idée a touch of

Une idée de gingembre: A suggestion, a touch of ginger.

un brin a bit

Un brin foufou: A bit scatty.

un tantinet a trifle

Un tantinet compliqué: A trifle complicated.

à volo as much as you want, as you wish (from 'volonté')

Tiens, regarde ça. Samedi soir, vin blanc à volo: Hey, look at that. Saturday night, white wine ad lib.

fou incredible (used for intensification)

Un monde fou: A great crowd.

Un fric fou: An incredible amount of money.

Quantity and intensification

à mort greatly, utterly

*Freiner **à mort***: To stand on the brakes.

à vapeur *
à plein tube * full blast

*Il a mis la sono **à plein tube***: He put the sound on full blast.

à tout crin through and through, full-blooded

*C'est un sportif **à tout crin***: He's an absolutely dedicated sportsman.

à tout-va full tilt

*Un professionnel **à tout-va***: A complete professional.

bon teint thorough, real, genuine, stolid

*Un Savoyard (de) **bon teint***: A faithful Savoyard.

bœuf terrific

*Un effet **bœuf***: A terrific effect.

carabiné stiff, hefty

*Je lui ai envoyé une lettre d'engueulade **carabinée***: I sent him a stinker.

*Un rhume **carabiné***: A filthy cold.

drôlement very, jolly

*Elle en est **drôlement** contente*: She's jolly pleased about it.

(c'est) vachement * it's damned …

*C'est **vachement** difficile*: It's dammed difficult.

archi *   extra, more than (intensifier like
                               'arch' of archangel, archbishop)

*C'est **archi**gardé:* Security is very tight.

***Archi**bondé:* Packed tight.

*Ils sont **archi**copains:* They are bosom pals.

un remède de cheval   a vigorous, ultra-tough remedy

en diable   a hell of a ..., terribly

*Un bricoleur **en diable**:* A terrific do-it-yourself fan.

*Ça fait jeune **en diable**!:* Talk about looking really young!

mentir comme on respire   to be a born liar

comme pas un/deux   better than anyone else, like
                               nobody's business

*Elle fait de bons petits plats **comme pas une**:* You really ought to taste
some of her dishes.

fleuve   lengthy, of great size, (running on
                               and on like a river)

*Un discours **fleuve**:* A very long speech.

maison *   big, special, almighty (In standard
                               French 'maison' = home-made
                               and rather special: 'une tarte
                               maison'.)

*Elle l'a gratifié d'une gifle **maison**:* She treated him to an almighty slap.

To Quarrel

la prise de bec   tiff
la bisbille   quarrel, bickering

To Quarrel

se chamailler	to row, to wrangle
se bouffer le nez *	to have a set-to
se crêper le chignon *	to have a good old row (women)

To Question

cuisiner quelqu'un *	to 'grill' someone, to quiz someone
tirer les vers du nez à quelqu'un	to interrogate someone, to extract answers from someone

*Ah, il n'a rien voulu te dire? Moi, je vais lui **tirer les vers du nez**!*: So he didn't want to tell you anything? I'll make him talk!

R

Recovery

se remettre d'aplomb	to recover, get back to normal

*Ce jour de repos m'a complètement **remis d'aplomb**:* I am fully back to normal again after that day off.

recharger ses accus	to recharge one's batteries (from 'accumulateur')
reprendre du poil de la bête	to pick up again (of people and things)

*Après quelques semaines difficiles la livre sterling **reprend du poil de la bête**:* After some difficult weeks the pound is recovering.

regonfler	to buck up, cheer up
retaper	
ravigoter	
requinquer *	
remonter le moral	
(à quelqu'un)	

*Ce qui me **ravigote** c'est une heure sur mon balcon:* What sets me up is an hour on my balcony.

*Lorsque je vais au cinéma, j'en sors tout **requinqué**:* When I go to the cinema I come out feeling great again.

Regrets

j'en aurais pleuré	I could have wept
s'en mordre les doigts	to regret

Je m'en mords les doigts: I'm kicking myself.

ne pas en faire une	not to be too upset/put out
maladie/une jaunisse	

*Si je ne gagne pas, je **n'en ferai pas une maladie**:* If I don't win I shan't be too upset.

Relations

le pépé	grandad
le pépère	
le papy	
la mémé	grandma
la mémère	
la mamie	
le frangin *	brother, bro
la frangine *	sister, sis

Relations

le fiston	son
le beauf *	brother-in-law (from 'beau-frère')
le tonton	uncle, uncs (children's language)
la tata	auntie (children's language)
les pièces rapportées *	in-laws

*Une grande réunion de famille avec **les pièces rapportées** présentes aussi:* A large family gathering with the in-laws there as well.

les vieux (m)	parents, old birds

Relationship/friendship

le copain (la copine)	pal, chum, mate
le copinage	chumminess, jobs for the boys
copiner	to be pally

*Le patron est mon cousin, mais je dois travailler dur. Il ne **copine** pas:* The boss is my cousin, but I must work hard. There are no friendly favours.

faire ami-ami avec	to chum up with

***Faites ami-ami avec** les touristes qui visitent la capitale:* Be nice and friendly with the tourists visiting the capital.

le pote *	mate, pal
avoir des atomes crochus avec quelqu'un	to hit it off with someone (owing to a common interest), to click with someone (There is no connection with the modern scientific sense of atom.)

*Hélas je **n'ai** guère **d'atomes crochus avec** Bernard:* Unfortunately Bernard and I don't really hit it off.

Reluctance/ refusal

se faire tirer l'oreille	to need coaxing
pas pour un empire!	not for all the tea in China!
des clous! *	not bloody likely!
tu peux toujours courir! *	you've got a hope! not a chance!
très peu pour moi! *	no way! no thank you! not on your nelly!

Appréhender un voleur? **Très peu pour moi!**: Stop a thief? Not on your life!

j'ai d'autres chats à fouetter	I have more important things to do

Repetition

seriner quelque chose à quelqu'un	to din something into someone

On se rappelle des conseils souvent **serinés**: One remembers bits of advice which have been so often impressed on one.

re-	again (used for repetition)

Après une heure j'ai crevé. **Re**-*problème deux heures plus tard*: After an hour I had a puncture. The same problem again two hours later.

rebelote	repeat performance, here we go again, the same thing again

On va supprimer une vingtaine de postes immédiatement. **Rebelote** *pour la basse saison*: Some twenty jobs are to go at once. Repeat performance for the low season.

Repetition

je connais la chanson   I've heard it all before

Oui, oui, les prix flambent; les temps sont difficiles. **Je connais la chanson**: Yes, yes, prices are shooting up; times are difficult. I've heard it all before.

c'est toujours la même ritournelle/rengaine   it's always the same old story

chanter toujours la même antienne   to harp on the same old theme

Reprimand

engueuler quelqu'un enguirlander   to blast someone

passer un savon à quelqu'un   to give someone a good rollicking

*Si vous continuez comme ça vous pouvez vous attendre à ce qu'***on vous passe un** *bon* **savon**: If you go on like that you can expect a good ticking-off.

sonner les cloches à quelqu'un   to give someone a rocket

en prendre pour son grade en prendre pour son rhume *   to get hauled over the coals

se faire taper sur les doigts   to get one's knuckles rapped

se faire attraper   to catch it, get into trouble, get what-for

Si je ne rentre pas tout de suite je vais me **faire attraper**: If I don't get back at once I'll get into trouble.

Reservation

il y a à prendre et à laisser
it's like the curate's egg, there's good and bad,

il y a à boire et à manger là-dedans
there are good things and bad things

Quel jugement portez-vous sur la scène pop? – **Il y a à prendre et à laisser***:* How do you rate the pop scene? – There are good things and bad things.

Resignation

faire avec
to make the best of something, to put up with something

J'ai toujours mes rhumatismes. Mais voilà, faudra **faire avec***!:* I've still got my rhumatism. Just have to put up with it!

encaisser
to suffer, go through it, take it

Ils **encaissent** *avec le sourire:* They lump it cheerfully.

Resourcefulness

se débrouiller
se démerder *
to cope, manage
(The French have a reputation for always being able to manage, to find a way.)

Eh bien, je vais **me débrouiller** *pour en trouver:* Well, I'll find some somehow.

débrouillard
resourceful

Pour faire ça il faut être courageux, bien sûr, mais **débrouillard** *aussi:* To do that, you must of course be brave, but you must also have your wits about you.

Resourcefulness

le système D *   the ability to cope, see a way
                                 through (from 'Débrouille')

se défendre   to cope, manage, look after
                                 oneself

*Il **se défend** pas mal:* He's getting on all right.

Responsibility/blame

porter le chapeau/le képi   to carry the can
payer les pots cassés
payer la casse

*Il y a sûrement une taupe qui est l'auteur de ces fuites. Alors on a tort,
à mon avis, de faire **porter le chapeau** au ministre:* There is surely a
mole behind these leaks. So it is wrong, in my view, to make the minister
carry the can.

renvoyer la balle   to pass the buck

être mouillé   to be involved, implicated

*Il est **mouillé** jusqu'au cou dans ce scandale:* He's up to his neck in this
scandal.

Restart

repiquer   to restart, go back (to something)

***Repiquer** à l'enseignement:* To go back to teaching.

Revenge

guetter/attendre quelqu'un to wait for the opportunity to get
au tournant   one's own back, to wait to catch
                                 someone out, to bide one's time

*En ce moment on me **guette au tournant**. On attend que je fasse quelque chose de stupide:* At the moment they are waiting to catch me out, waiting for me to do something silly.

il ne l'emportera pas au paradis	he'll catch it later
il ne perd rien pour attendre	he won't escape his comeuppance

Risk

faire le saut	to take the plunge
se mouiller	to get involved

*Il ne veut pas **se mouiller**:* He wants to stay clear. He is sitting on the fence.

risquer le paquet	to risk all, go the whole hog
être dans l'œil du tigre **être dans le collimateur**	to be in the firing line

*Après le débat on va me poser des questions. Je serai **dans l'œil du tigre**!:* After the discussion they are going to ask me questions. I shall be in the firing line!

Road accidents/driving

griller un feu rouge	to go through a red light
embrasser un platane	to go smack into a tree
se payer un quinze tonnes *	to have a collision with a heavy lorry
faire une queue de poisson à quelqu'un	to 'carve someone up'
faire un créneau	to slot into a parking space between two cars

Road accidents/driving

s'arrêter pile
piler (net)

to stop dead

*Un camion **s'arrête pile** devant nous:* A lorry stops dead right in front of us.

les conducteurs du soixante-quinze

Parisian drivers (from the Paris code number 75) (humorous/pejorative)

le chauffard

road hog

appuyer sur/écraser le champignon

to put one's foot down

le fou du volant

mad, wild driver

rouler idiot

to drive like a fool

*Ceux qui **roulent idiot** sur les autoroutes:* Those who indulge in motorway madness.

aller dans les décors

to go off the road and hit something

Il est allé dans les décors

le papillon	(parking) ticket
la contredanse *	(normally 'contravention')

Je retrouve ma bagnole et qu'est-ce que je vois? Un **papillon**!: I get back to my car and what do I see? A parking ticket!

faire sauter une contredanse	to get a summons lifted, cancelled, removed
le conducteur du dimanche	week-end driver (and a bad one)
rouler pépère **rouler à la papa**	to drive gently along, to meander along
cracher quelqu'un **vomir quelqu'un** *	to drop someone off

Tu me **craches** *ici, devant l'hôtel:* Drop me here, at the hotel.

Roughness/ violence

passer quelqu'un à tabac **tabasser quelqu'un**	to beat, rough someone up
le passage à tabac	beating up
une dérouillée **une raclée** **une trempe** * **une volée de bois vert**	thrashing, drubbing (also means severe criticism)
rentrer dans le lard à quelqu'un * **tomber sur le poil à quelqu'un**	to pitch into someone
un quarante-quatre maison *	a hefty boot (44 is the shoe size, the equivalent of 11)

Attention! Ou vous aurez mon **quarante-quatre** *dans le derrière:* Watch it! Or you'll get my boot up your backside.

To Run away/be off/vanish

se sauver   to run away

*Bon, **je me sauve**:* Right, I must fly.

filer   to be off, to scram

*Mon frangin **file** à l'hosto:* My brother makes tracks for the hospital.

se casser *   to run along, to split
se barrer *
se débiner *

***Barre-toi**, petit!:* Beat it, kid!

se tirer   to go away, to make off

*«Vous ne pouvez pas entrer», dit le videur. «**Tirez-vous**!»:* 'You can't come in', the bouncer said. 'On your way!'

se tailler *   to scarper
détaler

*Quand je vois arriver les soldats, je **me taille**:* When I see the soldiers coming I make myself scarce.

*Il a **détalé** sur sa moto:* He took off on his motor bike.

s'éclipser   to clear off
se calter *
déguerpir
se faire la malle *
se faire la paire *

*Il a saisi mon porte-feuille et **s'est fait la paire** avec:* He snatched my wallet and did a bunk with it.

lever le pied   to run away secretly, disappear

*Il a **levé le pied**:* He did a bolt.

mettre les voiles	to split
mettre les bouts	
les mettre *	

*Cinq heures. On **met les bouts**?*: Five o'clock. Shall we split?

prendre le large	(literally 'to put out to sea': a nautical expression)
piquer un cent mètres	to hare off

*Il a **piqué un cent mètres** olympique*: He ran off like a bat out of hell.

se cavaler	to skedaddle
se carapater	
ficher le camp	
foutre le camp *	(impolite usage)
prendre la clé des champs/	
la poudre d'escampette	

*Fiche-moi **le camp**!*: Get lost!

se volatiliser	to vanish
s'évaporer	
dégage!	scram! beat it!
du balai!	
du vent!	
disparaître de la circulation	to disappear from the scene
disparaître du paysage	
disparaître dans la nature	to vanish into thin air

S

School

Abbreviated words are a feature of familiar speech and of young people's speech in particular:

le dirlo	H.M. (from 'directeur')

School

le proto	head of a lycée (from 'proviseur')
l'instit	primary-school teacher (from 'instituteur')
le prof	teacher (from 'professeur'), master
le potache	schoolboy, pupil
bizuther	to bully (through initiation ceremonies)
le bizuthage	bullying (of new students)
sécher	to cut (school)

*De temps en temps je **séchais** le lycée:* I used to cut school at times.

fuguer	to do a bunk, to bunk off
coller quelqu'un	to put someone in detention
la colle	detention

*Deux heures de **colle** et je n'avais rien fait!:* Two hours' detention and I didn't do anything!

se faire virer	to get chucked out, expelled
la boîte **le bahut**	school
bûcher	to swot away
potasser (son français)	to work hard at (one's French)
le fayot	swot
un fort en thème	a studious type, a 'brain'
le cancre	'thickie'
le pion	outside student who performs prefect-style supervision duties
fayoter *	to suck up

le dico	dictionary
le porte-doc	briefcase (from 'porte-documents')
la récré	break (from 'récréation')
chahuter	to rag, be rowdy
le chahut	ragging, uproar
le bac **le bachot**	'baccalauréat' exam
la boîte à bachot	crammer's
cafarder **cafter**	to sneak

*Ici on ne **cafte** pas! Ne l'oublie pas!:* No telling tales here! Don't forget it!

les maths (f)	maths
la géo	geography

*Tu aimes **la géo**?:* Do you like geog?

l'antisèche (f)	crib (from 'sécher', when one's mind goes a complete blank)

Sea

la grande bleue	the (deep blue) sea
la mare aux harengs	the Atlantic (the herring pond)

Secrecy

je suis une tombe	my lips are sealed
en douce	on the quiet

*Ils l'ont piqué **en douce**:* They pinched it on the quiet.

*Il picole **en douce**:* He's a secret drinker.

Secrecy

mon petit doigt me l'a dit   a little bird told me

To Sell

bazarder   to flog, get rid of

*Alors, tu as **bazardé** ta bécane?:* So you've got rid of your bike?

To Settle down

s'acheter une conduite   to settle down (to a steady life)

se ranger (du côté) des   to settle down
voitures *

*Incroyable! Tu vas alors **te ranger des voitures**!:* I can't believe it! You are going to settle down then!

se tasser   to settle down

*Il doit laisser les choses **se tasser**:* He must let things settle down.

The opposite Sex

faire du plat à quelqu'un   to chat someone up

*Il a **fait du plat** à la jolie serveuse:* He chatted up the pretty waitress.

draguer (les filles)	to try to get off with, to make passes at (the girls)
ne penser qu'à ça **être porté sur la bagatelle**	to have sex on the mind
le démon de midi	middle-aged 'itch'
le cavaleur **le coureur**	womanizer
avoir quelqu'un dans **la peau** **en pincer pour quelqu'un**	to be smitten with someone

*Elle l'a **dans la peau**:* She's smitten with him.

avoir le/un ticket avec **quelqu'un**	to hit it off with someone

*J'ai **le ticket avec** la blonde!:* I'm getting on smashingly with the blond!

To Show up

se pointer	to show up

*Voilà! Les nuages **se pointent**!:* There you are! The clouds are appearing!

montrer son nez **pointer son nez**	to appear

*Dès qu'un flic **pointe son nez**, les gosses se sauvent:* As soon as a copper shows up the boys make off.

rappliquer	to turn up, come along, return, roll up
débarquer	to turn up, arrive, land

*Tu sais que Pierre vient de **débarquer** à Paris?:* You know that Pierre has just arrived in Paris?

To Show up

ne pas briller à l'horizon   not to show up, to be no sign of

*Les soldats ennemis **ne brillaient pas à l'horizon**:* There was no sign of the enemy soldiers.

Similarity/comparison

ou tout comme   or as good as (makes no difference)

*Il était disgracié **ou tout comme**:* He was disgraced or as good as.

le portrait (tout) craché   the spitting image

c'est du pareil au même   it comes to the same thing
c'est kif-kif (bourricot) *   ('kif-kif' comes from Arabic)
c'est bonnet blanc et blanc bonnet

(c'est) le jour et la nuit   there's no comparison, it's like chalk and cheese (of people and things)

*Pas de vin ordinaire aujourd'hui mais un vin de grand cru. **Le jour et la nuit**:* No table wine today but a vintage wine. Just no comparison.

les deux font la paire   they are two of a kind, they are a right pair

ça fait deux   we are miles apart, I don't understand a thing about it

*Les ordinateurs et moi, **ça fait deux**:* Computers and me, we are miles apart.

itou *   also, likewise

*Le salon est fort confortable et les chambres **itou**:* The sitting room is very comfortable, likewise the bedrooms.

*Et moi **itou**:* Same here.

idem   ditto

*Il faut payer pour y entrer. **Idem** pour les toutous:* You have to pay to go in. Ditto for four-legged friends.

Petites Révisions - Test Yourself!

PETITES REVISIONS 6
(Paris – Similarity/comparison)

Translations page 175

1. Le flic n'a pas été gentil et il m'a embarqué.
2. Sa peur n'est pas du cinéma, j'en suis archisûr.
3. Mon frangin dit que c'est vachement cher.
4. Quoi, y aller sans les potes? Très peu pour moi!
5. Mon petit doigt m'a dit qu'il s'est acheté une conduite.
6. Je fais le saut et je pars demain pour l'Europe.
7. Je ne dis pas que je roule pépère mais je ne suis pas un chauffard non plus.
8. Le mec a pris le large en me voyant.
9. Je me souviens qu'on chahutait les profs.
10. Il va me le donner – ou le prêter. C'est kif-kif.

Size

le malabar — hefty bloke

haut comme trois pommes — quite small

*Lorsque j'étais **haut comme trois pommes***: When I was just so high.

conséquent — large, sizeable

*Un chèque **conséquent***: Quite a hefty cheque.

hénaurme — enormous

interminable — immensely long (humorous)

*Et puis ce type descend de son **interminable** limousine*: Then this chap gets out of his 'stretched' limousine.

long comme ça — as long as your arm

*Il a des titres **longs comme ça***: He's got things after his name galore.

*Une voiture **longue comme ça**!*: One of those vast cars!

Skill

jouer comme une pantoufle
jouer comme un sabot
jouer comme un pied — to be a hopeless player

conduire comme un manche — to be a lousy driver

avoir la bosse (de quelque chose) — to have a flair, gift for something

*Il **a la bosse** des maths*: He has a maths brain.

avoir le compas dans l'œil   to have a good eye, to be a good judge of distance

*Il conduit avec maestria. Il **a le compas dans l'œil**:* He drives brilliantly. He has good judgement.

passer entre les gouttes   to steer clear of the difficulties that crop up (The image is of avoiding the showers.)

ne pas être manchot   to be no slouch, to be pretty skilful, to have one's wits about one (literally 'manchot' = one-armed)

(être) à la hauteur   to be up the mark, up to scratch

*Serez-vous à **la hauteur**?:* How will you stack up?

Speech/talk

un laïus*   speech, talk

*Il a présenté **un** petit **laïus** sur la viticulture:* He gave a little talk on wine growing.

dégoiser *   to prattle on, blab away

*Si tu veux savoir les potins va parler à la concierge. Elle **dégoise** sans arrêt:* If you're interested in gossip go and speak to the concierge. She's always blabbing.

tenir le crachoir *   to do all the talking, to hold forth

vider son sac   to say one's piece, what one has to say, to come clean

*Un journaliste a réussi à l'interviewer et il a **vidé son sac**:* A journalist managed to interview him and he told everything he knew.

Speech/talk

tailler une bavette
to have a chinwag, to have a gossip

discuter le bout de gras
to have a natter

c'est du vent
it's just empty talk, blether

et patati et patata *
et tout et tout
and so on, etcetera etcetera

*Elle voulait savoir s'il avait fait beau, si j'avais bien mangé **et patati et patata**:* She wanted to know if I had had good weather, if the food had been good and so on and so forth.

les messes basses *
whispering, mutterings

*Allez! allez! Pourquoi ces **messes basses**?:* Come! Come! What's all this whispering?

les stratèges du café du Commerce
pub politicians, armchair strategists ('du Commerce' is a common name for a café)

Speed

à la vitesse grand V
at great speed

en quatrième vitesse
with all speed (even though nowadays top speed may be in fifth gear)

*Je m'en suis occupé **en quatrième vitesse**:* I saw to it with all speed.

sur les chapeaux de roue
at high speed ('chapeau de roue' = hub cap)

*Les bandits ont démarré **sur les chapeaux de roue**:* The gangsters roared off at high speed.

à tombeau ouvert

at breakneck speed

*Je les vois filer **à tombeau ouvert**, même parfois par mauvais temps:*
I see them hurtling along even sometimes in bad weather.

Il file à tombeau ouvert

à fond de train
à plein gaz
à fond la caisse *

flat out

à toutes pompes *
à tout berzingue *

lickety-split

*J'ai descendu la côte **à tout berzingue**:* I came tearing down the hill.

foncer

to tear along

*L'ambulance **fonce**:* The ambulance tears along.

dare-dare

with haste, hotfoot

*Elle est rentrée **dare-dare**:* She came dashing back.

vite fait

very quickly, in no time (at all)

*Si c'était vrai il aurait reçu, **vite fait**, un coup de téléphone:* If it had
been true he would have got a phone call in no time.

en cinq secs

in a flash, in a trice

aussi sec

immediately, pretty sharp

Speed

illico (presto) *   straight off

*Je lui ai dit de m'apporter ça **illico presto**!:* I told him to bring me that pronto!

en deux temps trois   in two wags of a cow's tail
mouvements
en moins de deux

avant qu'on puisse dire ouf *before you know it

le lambin   slowcoach

lanterner   to dilly-dally

*Après avoir **lanterné** toute la journée près de la gare:* After mooching around all day near the station.

Sport

se faire coiffer au poteau   to get beaten at the post

finir dans un mouchoir   to be a close finish

Ils finissent dans un mouchoir

Ils jouent au foot

le foot
le ballon rond

soccer

le ballon ovale
l'ovale

rugger

Retiré maintenant de l'ovale, il passe son temps à voyager: Now retired from rugby he spends his time travelling.

le treiziste

rugby-league player

le quinziste

rugby-union player

la planche
la latte

ski

*Ces enfants skient bien mais ils ont des **lattes** aux pieds depuis longtemps:* Those children ski well but they've been used to it for ages.

le tire-fesses

ski-lift, tow-bar

le chrono

(recorded) time (from 'chronomètre' = stop watch)

*Du 160 **chrono**: incroyable!:* Clocked at an incredible 100 mph!

Sport

faire des pompes — to do press-ups

pousser de la fonte — to do weightlifting, to 'pump iron'

le sportif en chaise longue — armchair sportsman

Stomach

le bide
la brioche *
la bedaine
la panse — paunch, belly

La brioche de la quarantaine: Middle-age spread.

Success

le tube — hit

*Elle aimait danser sur les rythmes des derniers **tubes**:* She liked to dance to the latest hits.

faire un tabac — to be a howling success (show business)

faire un malheur — ('malheur' = misfortune, but see 'terrible' under *Excellence*)

*Elle chante aussi bien que jamais et son show a **fait un tabac** hier soir:* She sings as well as ever and her show was a smash hit last night.

casser la baraque — to bring the house down

le clou — big moment

*La surprise du chef fut **le clou** du dîner:* The high spot of the dinner was the chef's surprise.

To Suit

botter to suit

*Cette fille me **botte**:* I fancy that girl.

Surprise

ça alors! well I never! well I'm blowed!

ça pour une surprise, c'est une surprise! talk of a surprise!

**sidéré
estomaqué
soufflé** staggered, knocked back

*Si cela arrivait, j'en serais **soufflé**:* If that happened I'd be staggered.

en rester baba to be dumbfounded

époustouflant breathtaking

les bras m'en tombent I'm staggered, thunderstruck

*Quoi – ils ont perdu? Pas possible! **Les bras m'en tombent!**:* What – they lost? Can't be true! I'm staggered!

on aura tout vu! that's unbelievable! well I never! I'd never have believed it! whatever next!

*Pierre professeur! **On aura tout vu!**:* Pierre a teacher! Would you believe it!

(du) jamais vu! you've never seen the like!

*Un embouteillage **jamais vu!**:* You've never seen such a traffic jam!

Surprise

ça décoiffe!

breathtaking, stunning, mind-blowing (from the image of being blown about in an open car at speed)

L'acrobatie aérienne, **ça décoiffe!**: Stunt flying is a mind-blowing experience!

T

Temper/mood

être d'une humeur de chien
être de mauvais poil
être comme un crin

to be in a foul temper

prendre la mouche

to flare up, take offence

quelle mouche t'as piqué?

what's got into you? what's up with you?

être soupe-au-lait

to be likely to flare up, to be very touchy

Cesse de monter comme une **soupe au lait** *et écoute-moi*: Simmer down and listen to me.

se lever du pied gauche

to get out of bed on the wrong side

piquer une crise

to hit the roof

Mon père a **piqué une crise** *quand je lui ai dit que j'avais perdu mon chéquier*: My father hit the roof when I told him I had lost my cheque book.

être bien/mal luné

to be in a good/bad mood

avoir la pêche
avoir le moral
avoir la frite *

to be in fine fettle,
to be feeling great

*Quelques collègues se découragent mais lui c'est un battant. Il **a le moral**:* Some colleagues are losing heart but he's a fighter. He is not down.

la rogne

bad mood, ill temper (often used in conjunction with 'grogne' – see under *Grumbling*)

Thing

le machin
le bidule

thingmabob

le truc

thingmabob, thing

***Le truc** moche, c'est qu'on vous paie très peu:* The lousy thing is that you are not paid much.

*A part ton boulot, c'est quoi ton **truc**?:* Apart from your job, what's your scene?

Think

gamberger *

to reflect, think (up)

*Je **gamberge** un plan pour les aider:* I'm thinking up a plan to help them.

phosphorer *

to reflect

*Cette situation fort difficile nous fait **phosphorer**:* This very difficult situation sets our brains working.

Time

à six heures pile
à six heures tapant   at six on the dot

Ils sont toujours là à six heures pile: They're always there at six on the dot.

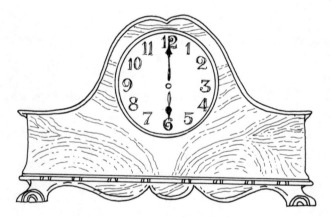

Six heures pile

ce mat *   this morning

A huit heures du mat: At eight in the morning.

cet aprèm *   this afternoon

un de ces quatre (matins)   one of these (fine) days

Un de ces quatre vous allez vous faire du mal: One of these days you are going to hurt yourself.

chaque jour que Dieu fait   every single day

Les pauvres! **Chaque jour que Dieu fait** *je pense à eux:* The poor things! Every single day I think of them.

arriver comme un cheveu/   to be inopportune, to turn up at
des cheveux sur la soupe   the wrong moment (remarks, people)

à perpète *   for ever (from 'à perpétuité')

On ne peut pas rester ici **à perpète**: We can't stay here for ever.

il y a belle lurette   donkey's years ago
ça fait un bail

J'y ai passé mes vacances en 1970 – **un bail**!: I spent my holidays there in 1970 – yonks ago!

il y a des lustres   ages ago, many moons ago (a lustrum is a period of five years)

Il y a des lustres *les Anglais connaissaient bien les casinos de la région:* Back in the past the English were regulars at the casinos around here.

ce n'est pas pour demain   it's not just round the corner

La retraite à cinquante ans, **ce n'est pas pour demain**: Retirement at fifty isn't just round the corner.

ce n'est pas demain la   it won't happen in a hurry
veille

Ce n'est pas demain la veille *que tout cela va changer:* All that is not going to change in a hurry.

tomber pile   to come at (just) the right time
tomber à pic
arriver à point nommé

l'heure tourne   time is ticking on

Time

à l'heure du laitier   at the crack of dawn ('laitier' = milkman)

Je quitte la maison **à l'heure du laitier** *et je me dirige vers la gare:* I leave home at the crack of dawn and head for the station.

passer un sale quart d'heure   to have a nasty time of it, to have some nasty moments, to go through a bad patch

primo   first(ly), for starters, to kick off with

secundo   second(ly)

tertio   third(ly)

Tired

crevé
claqué
flapi
éreinté
à plat   exhausted, all in (commonly used)

sur les rotules   ('rotule' = knee-cap)

Je les ai vus arriver – **crevés**, *fauchés, affamés:* I saw them arrive – dead tired, broke, hungry.

J'étais **sur les rotules**. *Je me suis écroulé dans le fauteuil:* I could hardly stand. I collapsed into the armchair.

être sur les dents   to be tired, harassed, under stress

le coup de pompe   feeling of tiredness

Le coup de pompe *de onze heures:* That 'mid-morning' feeling of fatigue.

Transport

la bagnole **la tire** *	car (much used word)

*Leur **bagnole** a été transformée en épave:* Their car was a write-off.

le bolide	fast car (literally 'bolide' = meteor)
la caisse * **la guimbarde** **le tape-cul** **le tacot**	banger, old car

*C'est un **tape-cul**:* It's a boneshaker

*La course de vieux **tacots**:* The old crocks' race.

la Deuche	Citroën 2CV (from 'deux chevaux')

*Qui n'est pas fier de sa **Deuche**?:* Who isn't proud of his 2CV?

le vélo **la bécane** **la petite reine**	cycle, bike

*C'est le roi de **la petite reine**!:* He's the cycling champ!

le VTT	mountain bike (from 'vélo tout terrain')
la mob **la moby** **le cyclo**	moped (from 'mobylette') (from 'cyclomoteur')
le petit/gros cube	small/big powerful motorbike
le mastodonte	juggernaught
le teuf-teuf	train, puffer
le zinc	plane, old crate

Transport

l'hélico (m)
le ventilateur

helicopter, chopper, whirly-bird

*Je n'ai pas vu **l'hélico** se poser:* I didn't see the chopper land.

le transat

liner (from 'transatlantique' = transatlantic liner)

le rafiaut

old boat, tub

faire du stop
lever le pouce

to hitch-hike, to thumb a lift (from 'auto-stop')

*Faute de fric j'ai dû **faire du stop**:* Being short of cash I had to hitch a lift.

aller à pince(s) *

to go on foot, to leg it

prendre le train d'onze heures *

to go on Shank's pony

être motorisé

to have transport, to be mobile

*Pour les visiteurs **motorisés** il n'y a pas de problème:* For visitors with their own transport there is no problem.

Type

l'acabit (m)

type, sort, ilk

*Que voulez-vous? Ils sont du même **acabit**:* What do you expect? They are of the same kind.

de tout poil

of all kinds, every sort

*Des touristes **de tout poil**:* Tourists of every sort.

U

Umbrella

le pébroque
le riflard *
le chamberlain *

umbrella, brolly

(from Neville Chamberlain, the
Prime Minister with his familiar
umbrella)

Le pébroque

Understanding

piger *
saisir

to understand, grasp

*T'as **pigé**?*: Got it?

*Je ne **saisis** pas:* I'm not quite with it.

je vous vois venir

I can see what you're getting at, I know what your game is

avoir un métro de retard

to be very slow on the uptake, to be lagging a long way behind

la jugeote

understanding, sense

**pour moi c'est du chinois/
de l'hébreu**

not a word do I understand (Chinese and Hebrew were apparently considered the difficult languages, whilst for us it was Greek and Dutch, as in 'double Dutch'.)

Unkindness

être vache *

to be nasty, a swine (much used word)

une peau de vache

a real so-and-so, a swine

**faire une crasse à
quelqu'un**

to play a mean, nasty trick on someone

*Un jour à l'école je lui ai **fait une crasse** et j'en rougis toujours:* One day at school I played a nasty trick on him and I still blush at the thought.

**c'est le coup de pied de
l'âne**

it's kicking a man when he's down

To Upset/thwart

chambouler
chambarder
to upset, scupper

*Il n'a pas envoyé l'argent, ce qui a **chamboulé** mes plans:* He didn't send the money, which scuppered my plans.

V

Vanity

faire de l'esbrouffe
faire de l'épate
faire le mariol
faire le malin
to show off, swank

*Ce n'est pas le moment de **faire le malin**:* It isn't the moment to try to be smart.

se croire
to be very pleased with oneself, conceited

*Mon Dieu! Qu'est-ce qu'il **se croit** celui-là!:* My Goodness! This one doesn't half fancy himself!

le frimeur
show-off

*Un chauffeur **frimeur**:* A show-off driver.

le m'as-tu vu
swank

s'envoyer des fleurs
to blow one's own trumpet, to pat oneself on the back

Vanity

ne pas avoir mal aux chevilles

to be self-satisfied, to pat oneself on the back (ironical – kicking one's ankles expresses satisfaction for compliments, congratulations)

t'as les chevilles qui enflent
ça va les chevilles?

don't boast so much, you're blowing your own trumpet

Victims

le gogo
le jobard
le pigeon

sucker

Un **pigeon** bon à plumer: A sucker who is a sitting duck.

Le cochon de payant

le cochon de payant	the one that doesn't get it for nothing, the poor bloke 'what' pays
une bonne pomme * **une bonne poire** *	a right old sucker
marcher	to fall for

Ils ont **marché**: They fell for it.

l'avoir dans l'os *	to have been caught out, tricked
le lampiste	the poor subordinate (who gets the blame and stands the racket)

W

Warning

ça nous pend au nez!	there's trouble coming our way!
trouver à qui parler	to meet one's match

Les chars ennemis **trouveront à qui parler**: The enemy tanks will meet their match.

faire gaffe *	to watch out
ça va barder	there's going to be trouble, there are going to be fireworks
il y aura du sport	there'll be some fun (ironical), some aggro, some 'bovver'
on verra de quel bois je me chauffe	they'll see what I'm made of
s'il me cherche, il me trouvera!	if it's trouble he wants, he is going to get it!

Warning

bonjour ... here comes, you can expect, watch out for ...

Un verre ça va, trois verres ... **bonjour** *les dégâts!:* One drink, well that's all right, but with three, you'll get more than a fright! (road-safety slogan)

Weather

tomber de la flotte * to rain heavily, come down, pour

Que disait ma grand-mère? «Soleil rouge du matin fait trembler le marin.» Et voilà, il **tombe de la flotte**!: What did my grandmother say? 'Red sky in the morning, shepherd's warning.' And there you are, it's pouring!

il pleut à seaux it's bucketing down

il pleut des hallebardes * it's raining cats and dogs
il pleut des cordes ('hallebardes' = spears)

Il pleut des cordes

se faire saucer   to get drenched

la gadoue   slush

il fait frisquet   it's nippy

Il y a un petit vent froid ce matin. **Il fait frisquet:** There's a chilly little wind this morning. It's nippy.

le fond de l'air est frais   it's chilly outside

il fait un froid de canard/ de loup   it's bitterly cold

Il fait un froid de canard *et je vais rester douillettement chez moi au coin du feu:* It's bitterly cold and I am going to stay snugly at home by the fireside.

ça caille *   it's brass monkey weather

il fait un temps de chien   it's vile weather

il fait un vent à décorner les bœufs   it's blowing great guns (enough to dehorn the oxen)

Work

je n'ai pas chômé   I've not been idle, I haven't sat around doing nothing (normally 'chômer' = to be unemployed)

galérer
ramer
bosser
trimer
cravacher   to work hard, slave away

J'ai **bossé** *comme un fou:* I worked like mad.

avoir du pain sur la planche   to have plenty of work in store, waiting to be done

Je ne manque jamais de **pain sur la planche**: I've always got plenty (of work) to do.

Work

aller au charbon to get down to it, to get down to hard work

sur le tas on the job

*Tout apprendre **sur le tas***: To learn it all on the job.

le boulot work, job (very commonly used)

*Il va de **boulot** en **boulot***: He goes from job to job.

l'assiette au beurre (f)
le fromage
la planque * nice, easy job, cushy number

*C'est une bonne **planque***: I've got it made in this job.

être sur la brèche to be hard at it, slogging away

des heures sup (f) overtime (from 'supplémentaire')

faire la plonge to do the washing-up (as in a restaurant)

les pluches (f) potato peeling, spud bashing

le bagne slaving away (like convicts), hard labour

*Après presque quarante ans de **bagne***: After slaving away for nearly forty years.

Worry

se faire du mouron to worry, upset oneself
se bouffer les sangs *
se faire du mauvais sang
se mettre martel en tête (from 'martel' = marteau = hammer)
se faire de la bile
se faire des cheveux
se casser la tête

Ne vous cassez pas la tête, *ce n'est pas tellement important:* Don't worry, it's not that important.

Pourquoi **se mettre martel en tête**? *Le pire n'arrive pas toujours:* Why worry? The worst doesn't always happen.

se faire un sang d'encre — to be worried to death

t'en fais pas! — don't let it worry you!

chiffonner — to upset, bother

Il y a toujours quelques détails qui me **chiffonnent**: There are still some details which niggle me.

j'te raconte pas l'angoisse — I can't tell you how worried I am

Il m'a demandé mes papiers, que j'avais laissés chez moi. **J'te raconte pas l'angoisse**: He asked for my papers, which I had left at home. You can imagine how worried I was.

Petites Révisions - Test Yourself!

PETITES REVISIONS 7
(Size – Worry)

Translations page 176

1. Il saute dans la bagnole et il démarre sur les chapeaux de roue.
2. C'est un grand malabar mais il joue comme une pantoufle.
3. Tout le monde parle de lui. Il fait un malheur.
4. Mais c'est toujours les lampistes – on le sait depuis belle lurette – qui subissent les conséquences.
5. Je suis claqué mais je serai là à six heures pile.
6. Je l'ai vu arriver sur son gros cube.
7. Il pleut des cordes et j'ai oublié mon pébroque!
8. J'attendais toujours. Je me bouffais les sangs.
9. «Il faut qu'on aille au charbon.» «C'est ça. Tu piges vite!»
10. Ne t'en fais pas. Je gamberge sérieusement pour les aider.

Petites Révisions - Translations

PETITES REVISIONS 1
(Abandonment – Cheap)

1. She crossed the desert on her own. No mean feat!
2. Instead of chucking it all in you worked hard and you are a millionaire. I take off my hat to you.
3. We'll go for a trip (walk, drive) on Sunday. Agreed?
4. I'm going to read a good thriller with nobody here to pester me.
5. The doc told me to stay in bed. That's really rotten.
6. Come on! Eleven o'clock. Time for bed. OK?
7. Monday tomorrow – and it's back to the commuter grind.
8. I don't want to see his slides. It's going to be deadly dull!
9. We are going to a (night) club. We are going to have fun.
10. Buy it! It's dirt cheap!

PETITES REVISIONS 2
(Children – Ease/facility)

1. 'Got a fag?' the kid asks me.
2. Don't forget your woolly and your mac.
3. I'm absolutely freezing here. I'll have a calvados to warm me up.
4. There's time to knock back a drink.
5. He got sloshed and this morning he's got a hangover.
6. No problem. It's a piece of cake!
7. I admire him; he does it all effortlessly.
8. We'll have a drink before going to the demo.
9. Finding the lost things won't be at all easy. That's the snag.
10. I think he is trying to lead me up the garden path. Meanwhile, not a word!

PETITES REVISIONS 3
(Efford – Food)

1. It'll cost you the earth.
2. I am mad on tennis and one day I invited her to come to Wimbledon with me. Nothing doing!
3. You go if you want to but I'm not keen.
4. Great! We are going skiing. The snow is super.
5. It's stodgy food. Frankly, I'm fed up with it.
6. I'm going to miss my train. That would be the last straw!
7. I was frightened as I came down the slope especially when I took a tumble.
8. You are chickening out? We've had it then.
9. We'll have a little snack before going out.
10. The nosh will be good, that's certain.

PETITES REVISIONS 4
(To play the Fool – Impatience)

1. One can get in free. He told me so for the umpteenth time.
2. There is nothing to make a fuss about. But he always wants to grumble.
3. I've tried umpteen times to stop smoking.
4. 'All well?' he said to me as always.
5. Of course we must go round the museums. But there's no rush!
6. I hung around for a time but nobody came.
7. After the accident I went to see him at his place. Fortunately he wasn't hurt.
8. I begin to feel a bit hungry so I go back home.
9. What a cold wind! We'll catch our death!
10. I'm not going there. I don't feel too marvellous this morning.

PETITES REVISIONS 5
(Impertinence – Opportunity)

1. They are waiting fo the VIPs to go.
2. To my surprise he used a four-letter word to him.
3. That interests me. It's up my street.
4. You can't get in without showing your identity papers.
5. I was lucky. My cousin knows the ropes and he gave me some tips.
6. This hundred-franc note is for me!
7. It helps me to earn my living.
8. He told me he was broke.
9. You must jump at the chance if you've enough lolly.
10. This time he has really boobed.

PETITES REVISIONS 6
(Paris – Similarity/comparison)

1. The cop wasn't very nice and he nabbed me (pulled me in).
2. His fear is for real. I'm dead certain of it.
3. My brother says it's damned expensive.
4. What, go there without my mates? Not on your life!
5. A little bird told me that he has settled down.
6. I am taking the plunge and I leave tomorrow for Europe.
7. I don't say I just toddle along gently but I am not a roadhog either.
8. The bloke scarpered on seeing me.
9. I remember we ragged the teachers.
10. He is going to give it to me, or lend it. It's the same thing.

PETITES REVISIONS 7
(Size – Worry)

1. He jumps into the car and starts off at speed.
2. He's a big hefty bloke but he's a useless player.
3. Everyone is talking about him. He's a big hit.
4. But it's always the underlings – as has been known for ages –who suffer the consequences.
5. I'm dead beat but I'll be there at six on the dot.
6. I saw him arrive on his big motorbike.
7. It's raining cats and dogs and I've forgotten my brolly.
8. I was still waiting. I was getting pretty worried.
9. 'We'll have to get down to hard work!' 'That's right. You catch on quickly!'
10. Don't worry. I'm thinking hard how to help them.